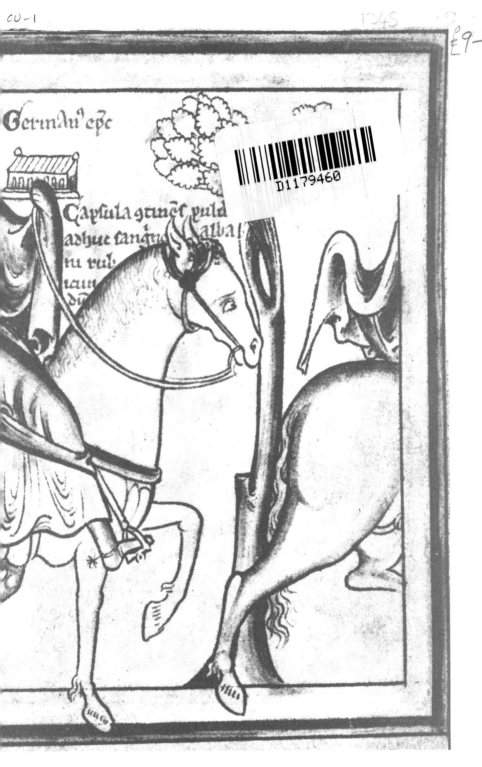

blood of the martyr Alban. From the thirteenth century Book of St Alban, Matthew Paris.

Trinity College, Dublin

THE EARLY CHURCH
IN EASTERN ENGLAND

by

MARGARET GALLYON

TERENCE DALTON LIMITED
LAVENHAM . SUFFOLK
1973

Published by
TERENCE DALTON LIMITED
S B N 900963 19 0

Printed in Great Britain at
The Lavenham Press Limited
Lavenham   Suffolk

Contents

Index of Illustrations

Preface

England in the early Anglo-Saxon period was divided into seven major kingdoms. This book deals only with the four south eastern kingdoms, Kent, Sussex, East Anglia and Essex, with an additional chapter on St Guthlac, who belonged to Middle Anglia, a small kingdom between East Anglia and Mercia.

Unless otherwise stated all quotations from Bede's *Ecclesiastical History* are from Leo Sherley-Price's translation. His spellings of names are also used. I have not thought it necessary to give footnote references to all these quotations.

I wish to express my gratitude to the many people who have helped me with the writing of this book, in particular to those who have written to me about various aspects of it, to the Cambridge libraries for allowing me extended loans of books, to Miss Nancie Pelling for drawing the map, to Mrs Margaret Pike for typing the manuscript, to E. E. Swain of Hunstanton for their expert photographic work and advice, to Miss Joan Liversidge for reading the chapter on Roman Britain, to Professor Dorothy Whitelock, Canon T. C. Heritage and Mr John Dawson for reading the typescript and offering many useful suggestions, and finally to my family for their generous help and encouragement.

Eastern England in Early Anglo-Saxon Times   *Nancie Pelling*

Introduction

ALTHOUGH the main purpose of this book is to examine the introduction of Christianity to east and south east England in the sixth and seventh centuries it would be misleading to suggest that the Faith first reached this island at that time. Certainly the seventh century saw a remarkable upsurge of missionary activity in Britain, both from the Continent and from the Celtic Church in Ireland, but there is evidence that it was preached and practised in various parts of Britain long before that time, when the country was a province of the Roman Empire.

Britain had been invaded by Roman legions in AD 43 in the time of the Emperor Claudius. The establishment of their base at Richborough in Kent and their advance northwards towards Colchester was the beginning of an occupation of Britain which was to last for almost four centuries. Ordered government and material prosperity followed in the wake of the invaders and everywhere their skill as architects, road builders and engineers became apparent. A series of well constructed roads, remains of which survive to this day, linked important military and administrative centres and massive fortifications and defensive walls lined Britain's coasts and frontiers. Towns of all sizes sprang up, the more important with their public baths, fora, shops and temples. The finest temple in first century Roman Britain was that built in honour of the Emperor Claudius at Camulodunum (Colchester) capital of the province at that time. On country estates fine stone villas were built with under-floor heating; walls were decorated with frescoes and floors with mosaics.

The Roman occupation of Britain continued until the early years of the fifth century when troops were evacuated for deployment in other parts of the Empire. The withdrawal of soldiers, administrators, civic officials and experts in various fields led to a gradual disintegration of the civilization and culture which the Romans had brought to the country. The waning of their influence was finally sealed when the native population, the Romano-British, were confronted by a new set of invaders, the

Anglo-Saxons from the Continent who brought with them their own distinctive culture, so strikingly different from that of the Romans. But there remained from the years of the Roman occupation of Britain a spiritual heritage which, here as elsewhere, was to survive the crumbling of the Empire and which was never to be completely obliterated from the British scene. This was the Christian religion.

In addition to Christianity, a wide variety of religions were practised in Britain as in other parts of the Empire. A particularly popular faith among soldiers and traders and the higher ranks of Roman society was Mithraism, a mystery religion of Persian origin. It was abhorred by the Christians, perhaps because of its shadowy resemblance to some aspects of their own Faith. It was believed that Mithras had been born from a rock. He was depicted as a youth of splendid physique, a god of light who slew the bull for the world's salvation. Tertullian, a Christian of North Africa, writing in the early part of the third century, described the cult's ritual meal as a "devilish imitation of the Eucharist." Perhaps a major reason for the religion's failure to survive was its exclusively male appeal; no woman was allowed to participate in the worship of Mithras. A temple devoted to the god was discovered in 1953 on the bank of the Walbrook in London. Among the finds associated with the cult was a beautifully carved marble head, thought to represent Mithras and to have been part of a larger group, depicting the slaying of the bull.

Jupiter, Mercury, Venus, and other gods of classical mythology were worshipped in Roman Britain as is evidenced by the numerous statuettes which have been found during excavations of Roman sites. Most of our local museums have examples of these images on display. Although loyal Roman subjects were expected to pay outward homage to these deities many regarded them with intellectual scepticism and wavering trust for they were remote from the affairs of men and offered no solutions to the mysteries of life and death, good and evil.

The obligatory cult of emperor worship was equally powerless to touch men's hearts and to stir their wills to moral action. At best it encouraged an appreciation of the benefits of Roman government and gave some kind of unity to a sprawling empire. At worst it was responsible for the torture and death of thousands of Roman subjects, who, like the Christians, refused to worship the emperor as a god.

In sharp contrast to the inanimate gods of paganism the Christians claimed to worship a God who was alive and active in history. He was the Creator of the universe and the Father of all mankind. His attitude to man was not one of remote detachment and unconcern but one of involvement and love, and to make this love known to man he entered the human situation in the person of his Son, Jesus Christ. Converts to the Faith were not asked to pay homage to a mythical figure of the past, a Mercury, Mars or Mithras. Jesus was a recent figure of history, a man of their own time; thousands could recall his deeds and words, and the teaching of his followers bore the stamp of authority and personal conviction. To them he was truly man, but more, he was the Son of God, the long-awaited Messiah sent into the world to redeem his people. In this respect he transcended history and stood out among his fellows not only as a man excelling in every virtue possible to man, but as the author of man's eternal salvation. To all he offered the forgiveness of sins and the promise of eternal life. The religion which he founded had universal significance and drew within its bounds all classes of men: Roman and Barbarian, Jew and Gentile, slave and freeman, male and female, rich and poor. It excluded none, for all were potential beneficiaries of Christ's atoning death.

Christianity was, too, a religion which appealed both to the learned and the unlearned. It possessed a simplicity and directness which enabled the untutored peasant to grasp its essential teaching but also it possessed a depth and profundity which appealed to the minds of scholars and philosophers. Its heritage of Jewish writings, its records of the life and teaching of Jesus, its doctrines of God and the Church afforded a wealth of raw material to exercise the minds of thoughtful men. But unlike abstract speculative philosophy Christian philosophy was bounded by certain irrefutable historical facts and essential dogmas which were an integral part of the Faith. Around these an unlimited amount of theology could be built. From the time of St Paul, who possessed not only a burning zeal for the salvation of souls, but also a powerful intellect with which to present the Faith in rational terms, there followed men of outstanding qualities of mind, who devoted their gifts to the service of Christ and his Church, and became renowned for their skill as exponents of the Gospel and writers of theological works. Unlike the competitive religions of the day, Christianity insisted on the importance of sound doctrine and clear statements of belief.

Christ, by his enlightened attitude to women, enhanced the dignity of womanhood, setting a new standard for future attitudes; the New Testament and other early Christian writings provide evidence that women joined the Church from all ranks of society, benefitting it by the exercise of their own particular gifts. Children too were seen in a new light; their humility and faith were to be a pattern for adult man, and upon all who had dealings with the young rested a grave responsibility to avoid all occasions of causing them to err. Throughout its history the Church has been a pioneer in educating the young and imparting to them the truths of the Faith.

Christianity was essentially a missionary faith; it insisted on the duty of its adherents to propagate the Gospel, "Go forth to every part of the world, and proclaim the Good News to the whole creation" had been the Founder's last command to his followers.* Their obedience to this command was to result in the spreading of the Faith to all parts of the Roman Empire by the end of the first century. Eusebius, Bishop of Caesarea in AD 314, refers, in his *History of the Church,* to a widely held belief that to each of the apostles was allotted a portion of the world where he was to preach the Gospel.† Though there is no sound evidence for the truth of this notion it is certain that the apostles travelled far and wide for the purpose of propagating their Faith and so were true to their missionary vocation.

The precise means by which Christianity first reached Britain is not known. No record survives of missionary activity during the Roman occupation and the literary and archaeological evidence for the existence of Christian communities in Britain at that time is slender, though sufficient to make their presence a certainty. But we must bear in mind that in every epoch of Christian history the Faith has been spread not only by those celebrated saints whose names have been recorded and preserved, but also by countless unknown men and women, who have conveyed it to others by their work and their witness. In the chapters that follow a few outstanding figures of the early Church in Britain have been singled out for study, but there must have been innumerable others whose names are not known but who made their contribution towards the conversion of the island.

---

*Mark, chapter 6, verse 15.

†Eusebius. Book 3.

We may surmise that the Faith was brought to Britain in the first and second centuries by a variety of people in different walks of life; by clerics from the Continent; by travellers and traders from Gaul, Italy, Greece and the eastern Mediterranean countries; by immigrant Roman officials who for military, civic or other purposes settled in Britain with their families and servants, the latter being among the most enthusiastic adherents to the new religion. Tradition associates Glastonbury in Somerset with the earliest Christian church in Britain. The tradition stems from the writings of the twelfth century monk and historian William of Malmesbury who visited Glastonbury and studied ancient inscriptions, manuscripts and charters connected with its history. He firmly believed that the little wattled church at Glastonbury was the oldest in England and he wrote a treatise about its antiquity. When in 1184 the church and monastery were destroyed by a great fire and grants were subsequently made by Henry II for its restoration, enthusiasts revised William of Malmesbury's treatise, adding new and legendary material to it, connecting the founding of the monastery with Joseph of Arimathea, the honourable councillor of the Gospels who buried the body of Jesus. Joseph, it was claimed, had come to Britain with twelve companions to preach the Faith. He was given land at Glastonbury where he built a simple church and from this centre he evangelized the inhabitants of south west Britain. By including this legend in Glastonbury's history the fame of the church and abbey was revivified and its future glory ensured. Excavations have confirmed that the site was occupied in Roman times and literary evidence exists for the building of a church there by King Ine of Wessex towards the end of the seventh century, but the site on which he built was already at that time invested with an aura of sanctity because of its earlier associations with Christianity.

This chapter does not purport to give a comprehensive list of the literary and archaeological evidence for the existence of Christianity in Roman Britain, but several outstanding pieces of evidence have been selected.* We find for instance a reference to Christianity in Britain as early as AD 200 in the writings of Tertullian. He enumerates those places where the Faith of Christ had been preached and includes in the list "parts of Britain which, though

---

*For a full treatment of the subject see *Christianity in Roman Britain*, J. M. C. Toynbee. J.B.A.A. XVI 1953.

inaccessible to the Romans, have yielded to Christ."* Eusebius includes in his *History of the Church* the transcript of a letter written by the Emperor Constantine to the bishop of Syracuse informing him of a synod to be held at Arles in AD 314 and summoning the bishops of the Western Church to attend. Among the bishops present at the synod were three from Britain: Eborius from York, Restitutus from London and Adelphius from either Colchester or Lincoln, the latter bishop being accompanied by a priest and a deacon. The presence of British bishops at this and at other ecclesiastical conferences of which we know, implies that there was a thriving and well organized Church in Britain at the time and that it was sufficiently influential for its leaders to be invited to participate in theological debate on an international level.

Students of the early Church in Britain cannot begin to approach their subject without reference to the writings of Bede, monk and scholar of the twin monasteries of Monkwearmouth and Jarrow in Northumberland. In his book, the *Ecclesiastical History of the English People,* Bede traces the growth and development of Christianity in Britain from the time of the Roman occupation until the year AD 731 when he completed his work. It was written towards the end of his life — he died in 735 — by which time he had accumulated a great deal of knowledge about the early Church. Though historians have detected occasional inaccuracies in his writings and some have viewed with suspicion the more incredible of the miracles which he recounts, there is little doubt that Bede was a truthful and accurate historian with a concern to edify his readers and to give them reliable information about the spread of the Faith to various parts of Britain. He gathered his material from a variety of sources: from the writings of earlier historians, from chroniclers, hagiographers, from official records, letters and documents and from the researches of his own personal friends and acquaintances. In the Preface to his *History,* and scattered throughout the text, Bede frequently cites the exact source of his information about particular people, places and events. He names three Christians, though he says there were many others, who suffered martyrdom in Britain during the Roman occupation. Two of these names, Aaron and Julius, he learned from the writings of the sixth century British monk Gildas. The third, Alban, was a

---

*Tertullian. *Adversus Judaeos*. Chapter 7.

better known saint whose endurance and death were the subject of an early literary work, the *Passio Albani,* used by Bede as the basis of his own account of the saint's martyrdom. Many legendary accretions surround the story of Alban and the date of the martyrdom is not at all certain. Bede places it during the wave of persecution which occurred in 304 under the Emperor Diocletion but early evidence suggests that persecution did not reach Britain at that time. The earliest version of the *Passio Albani* ascribes the death of the saint to the period of persecution which took place under the Emperor Severus who governed from 193 to 211.* The main substance of the tradition concerning the martyrdom however can be regarded as both historical and trustworthy.

The story is a familiar one. Alban was a pagan, possibly a Roman soldier, living in the Roman municipium of Verulamium close to the present day St Albans. A Christian priest from Gaul, who was being pursued by his persecutors, found sanctuary at Alban's house and while there continued as usual his religious devotions. Observing the priest at his prayers and vigils Alban felt strongly drawn to the Faith which the priest practised and after receiving instruction he affirmed his faith in Christ and renounced his allegiance to pagan gods. When eventually the Roman persecutors discovered the priest's hiding place they came to arrest him and to lead him away for questioning but Alban who had given him protection thus far was determined to save his friend's life. He seized the priest's clerical garment, a cloak, distinctive of his office, wrapped it around himself and in this disguise gave himself up in place of his guest. When Alban was brought before the magistrate for interrogation his trick of deception was discovered. "If you wish to know the truth about my religion, know that I am a Christian," said Alban.† His refusal to sacrifice to pagan gods led to the infliction of tortures upon him and finally to his execution. He was beheaded in front of a vast crowd of onlookers in a place appropriate to a martyr's death, a hill where many kinds of wild flowers grew. It was close to Verulamium's fine arena, remains of which still stand today.

Excavations at Verulamium have revealed much of the ancient Roman town including the theatre built in a most attractive setting in undulating countryside and close to the Watling

---

*Bede's *Ecclesiastical History of the English People*. Colgrave and Mynors.
†Bede.

Street, an important Roman road, now the A5, linking Dover with Wroxeter and passing through London and St Albans. The theatre was in use from the middle of the second century until the end of the fourth century when it was abandoned and subsequently used for depositing rubbish. It may well be that the advance of Christianity had caused the decline of the theatre as a place of entertainment. The dances, mimes, pantomimes and gladiatorial fights performed in the Roman arenas were notorious for their vulgarity and cruelty and were denounced and shunned by the Christians. "We have nothing to do, in speech, sight or hearing, with the madness of the circus, the shamelessness of the theatre, the savagery of the arena, the vanity of the gymnasium," wrote Tertullian in his *Defence of Christianity.* *

Bede tells us that when the wave of persecution had abated a church of most beautiful workmanship was erected on the site of the martyrdom and that in his own day it was renowned for the many miracles that occurred at the saint's shrine. Devotion to St Alban persisted throughout the Middle Ages and prompted pious folk to make pilgrimages to his shrine. Remains of the shrine, elaborately carved and painted with scenes from the saint's martyrdom, can be seen in the present Abbey Church of St Albans. It dates from the fourteenth century.

The year 314 marked a turning point in the history of the Christian Church for then the Emperor Constantine issued a decree, known to us as the Edict of Milan, commanding the persecution of Christians to cease. He had been favourable towards the Christians since his rise to power in 306 but shortly before the edict, and when he was engaged in a military campaign against his enemy, Maxentius, he saw in a vision the Cross superimposed over the sun and bearing the inscription IN THIS CONQUER. His decisive victory at the Milvian Bridge served to confirm his faith in the Christian God and thereafter persecution of Christians ceased. Christianity was no longer an underground movement. It emerged into the light of day, proclaimed its message openly and held its services of worship in churches which by the command of the Emperor were restored to Christian communities.

Bede mentions churches in Britain which were used for worship in Roman times. One of these was St Martin's on the east side of Canterbury. We shall see in Chapter 2 that this church was

---

*Tertullian. *Apologeticus*. Chapter 38. Translated T. R. Glover.

restored in the early Anglo-Saxon period and used by the Christian Queen Bertha of Kent and by Augustine and his monks. The present church is of great antiquity and incorporates in its fabric a large amount of Roman bricks and masonry which may have formed part of the original church to which Bede refers. He describes a second church in Canterbury which was in use in Roman times and on the site of which stands the present Cathedral of Christchurch. Augustine restored it at the end of the sixth century when he came to England to convert the pagan English, dedicating it to Christ our Saviour. These two churches where Romano-British Christians worshipped must have been typical of many others up and down the country and future builders were to make good use of the masonry which survived.

The contribution which archaeology has to make towards the unravelling of the past is becoming increasingly appreciated and in this field great advance has been made in recent years. Not only are archaeologists applying modern scientific techniques to the examination of their discoveries but their work is being done in co-operation with experts in other fields: historians, geologists, palaeographers and so on.

In addition to the important archaeological discoveries made by experts during organized excavations other finds are often made quite by chance. It is not unusual for instance to hear of discoveries being made by farmers, roadworkers or builders during the course of their manual work. Such a discovery was made in 1962 during the construction of a ring road round Canterbury, when a hoard of fourth century silver spoons was unearthed, buried perhaps by its owners during troublous times and in the expectation of returning later to retrieve it. Two of the spoons are clearly marked with Christian symbols which indicates that the owner, or perhaps a member of his family, may have held Christian beliefs, but of course this evidence is not conclusive. A far more lavish find was made in 1946 when agricultural workers were ploughing a field near Mildenhall in west Suffolk not far from Icklingham, the site of an important Roman settlement, and unearthed a superb collection of fourth century silverware including plates, dishes, bowls, goblets and spoons, three of the latter also bearing the Christian symbols.

These symbols which appear on a number of Roman antiquities are mainly of two types. There is the Chi-Rho monogram which comprises the first two letters of the Greek word Christos, usually arranged ⳩ and the Alpha-Omega symbol, the first and last letters of the Greek alphabet. The use of this symbol owes its origin to the book of Revelation. " 'I am Alpha and Omega' says the Lord God, who is and who was and who is to come, the Sovereign Lord of all.'"* The symbols were widely used throughout the Empire as a sign of allegiance to Christ, the Chi-Rho monogram being inscribed on the helmet of the Emperor Constantine himself and incorporated into the design of his imperial standard. The symbols appear on a variety of objects which have been unearthed in Britain; on a leaden tank for instance, discovered on the site of the Roman villa at Icklingham, Suffolk, and now in the British Museum. Like other tanks of a similar type it may have been used for Christian baptism.

A particularly impressive example of the Chi-Rho symbol is to be seen on a mosaic pavement discovered in 1963 at Hinton-St-Mary in Dorset by workmen who were digging post holes for a new building. They accidentally uncovered a small section of what turned out to be an exceptionally fine and well preserved fourth century Roman pavement, now on display in the British Museum. At one end is the bust of a man of striking appearance, behind his head the Chi-Rho monogram and on either side pomegranates, symbolising in Graeco-Roman mythology, eternal life. The pavement has, without doubt, Christian significance but precisely who the bust represents is less certain. Professor Toynbee is of the opinion that it represents Christ.† Whether this is so or not, it is certain that the sacred emblem would have had no meaning for a pagan and that the owner of the villa or members of his household most likely held Christian beliefs.

Another villa with Christian associations was discovered at Lullingstone on the river Darenth in Kent. Three of the rooms were converted and re-decorated at the end of the fourth century for use as places of Christian worship. In the room designed to serve as a chapel, a series of six human figures were painted on the west wall; they were standing with arms outstretched in an attitude of prayer, the orante attitude, commonly adopted by early Christians. In this same room the south wall was decorated with a large painting

---

Revelations, chapter 1, verse 8.

† *The Christian Roman Mosaic. Hinton-St Mary, Dorset.* J. M. C. Toynbee.

of the Chi-Rho monogram. There is ample evidence that pagan gods were also worshipped in the villa, perhaps by the same family before its conversion to Christianity or by members of the household who clung to their traditional pagan beliefs.*

Future excavations may well reveal a great deal more evidence than we now possess for the existence of Christianity in Roman Britain. Buried beneath our cities, towns, and villages, our gardens, fields and pastures may lie hidden, objects of Christian significance or remains of Christian churches which will one day come to light and add to our knowledge of the early Church in Britain. To the layman, if not to the expert, the belief that potential knowledge awaits discovery by the archaeologist's spade or the farmer's plough is one of the chief reasons for the fascination of the subject.

But even a cursory look at the Roman exhibits in the museums up and down the country will make one aware of the scarcity of Christian compared to pagan religious relics. A showcase may exhibit numerous figurines of pagan deities but only a single item of Christian significance. It is important to remember in this connection that the Christian religion had grown up out of Judaism which forbade the worship of images and Christ himself had spiritualized even further the Jewish conception of God. "God is spirit," he had said, "and they that worship him must worship him in spirit and in truth."† Paul had condemned the worship of images in the city of Athens and challenged by his preaching the worshippers of the goddess Diana at Ephesus. "He is telling them that gods made by human hands are not gods at all," said Demetrius the chief silversmith who gained his living by making images of the goddess.‡ Not only were life-size images of the pagan deities put into the temples built in their honour, but replicas of them were made for household and personal use. Little wonder then that such a quantity of these images have survived.

Finally Christianity is known to have been practised in Roman Britain from the evidence of the presence of heretics in the country whose teaching was corrupting the Church. By the early part of the fifth century the heresy of Pelagius had spread to such

---

*Lullingstone Roman Villa. H.M.S.O. publication.

† John, chapter 4, verse 24.

‡ Acts, chapter 19, verse 26.

an extent in Britain that it was causing concern among Church leaders on the Continent. The heresy had originated from the teaching of Pelagius, born in Britain in about 354. He studied law in Rome, became a priest and attracted a number of followers who shared in propagating his erroneous beliefs. These, in essence, denied the doctrine of original sin and man's need of divine grace. "A man can be without sin if he choose," asserted Pelagius.* But this was contrary to the teaching of Christ and to that of St Paul who claimed "by God's grace I am what I am." Augustine, Bishop of Hippo in north Africa, was an ardent opponent of the heresy, for his own personal experience of deliverance from sin had convinced him of man's dependence upon God's grace in his efforts to achieve moral goodness. But Pelagius's teaching gained wide popularity especially among wealthy aristocratic families whose high rank and material prosperity produced in them an attitude of arrogant self-sufficiency and whose pride in the achievements of Rome gave them faith in the supremacy of man.

We know little of how the heresy reached Britain which was one of its major strongholds. Bede merely states that it was introduced into the country by Agricola, the son of a Pelagian bishop. It is likely that it was spread also by followers of Pelagius for they are known to have travelled far and wide for the purpose of disseminating their doctrine. It is possible too that Pelagius himself, as a young man and while still in Britain, had rejected the orthodox Faith and influenced British Christianity by his heretical views for he did not begin his studies in Rome until he was almost thirty years old. We shall see in the following chapter what steps were taken by the Church to rid Britian of this heresy and to restore it to orthodoxy.

---

*Documents of the Christian Church. H. Bettenson.

The Pagan English

WE HAVE referred in the Introduction to the decline of Roman influence in Britain after the withdrawal of troops, administrators and civic officials at the beginning of the fifth century, a decline which was accelerated by the advent of a new race of invaders who brought with them to Britain their own distinctive customs, culture, language and religious beliefs. These invaders were the Angles, Saxons and Jutes, later to be united under the one name, the English, and to give their name to the land they conquered, England or Engle-land. They were of Germanic origin, their homes in Frisia, north Germany and the Cimbric peninsular. Their advance against Britain occurred in three stages; we see them first as occasional raiders, then as invited mercenaries and finally as conquerors and settlers.

As early as the third century marauding bands of these Anglo-Saxon warriors from the Continent had made sporadic attacks upon Britain's eastern and southern shores, not yet for the purpose of setting on the land, but to rob it and carry off the spoil to their homelands. Against such attacks the Romans had built a number of defensive forts at strategic places on the east and south coasts, near to river estuaries or vital harbours where the Saxons might attempt to land. They were built at Brancaster, Burgh Castle, Walton Castle, Bradwell, Reculver, Richborough, Dover, Lympne, Pevensey, and Porchester, the stout outer walls of many still remaining. In Roman times they were garrisoned by infantry and cavalry troops and in nearby harbours were galleys prepared to intercept Saxon raiding ships. The forts were partially deserted after 367 when the officer in charge, the Count of the Saxon Shore, was killed during a concerted attack upon Britain by the Picts and Saxons. We shall see later that some of the forts were used in the seventh century as the sites for monastic settlements.

When the Roman Emperor Honorius officially broke the link between Rome and Britain in 410 telling the city states to see to their own defence it is likely that he foresaw a future reclamation of this most western province of the Empire; but their withdrawal left Britain in a vulnerable position for she had no organized and trained army comparable to that of the Romans. Her enemies, the Picts, from what is now Scotland and the Scots from Ireland, were quick to take advantage of her lack of military expertise and launched fierce attacks against her. Twice the Romans responded to appeals from the Britons and sent troops to assist in repelling the Picts and Scots but after this they left Britain, never to return. As well as harassment from the north and west, Britain was continually troubled by raids on her southern and eastern shores by the Anglo-Saxons.

It is to this transition period between the decline of Roman influence and the beginning of the Anglo-Saxon settlements that the two visits of Germanus of Auxerre to Britain belong, the first in 429, the second in 446. His purpose in coming to Britain was to combat the Pelagian heresy which was corrupting the British Church. A biography of the saint was written in about 480 by Constantius, a priest of Lyons. He tells how Germanus as a young man followed a secular career winning wide renown as a lawyer and later as military commander of his province in France. At the height of his fame he turned to religion with such fervour that "he deserted the earthly militia to be enrolled in the divine; the pomps of this world were trodden under foot; a lowly way of life was adopted; his wife was turned into a sister; his riches were distributed among the poor and poverty became his ambition."* He was consecrated Bishop of Auxerre in 418.

When in 429 the British Church appealed to the bishops in France for help in combating the Pelagian heresy Germanus was unanimously selected by the synod. He came to Britain with a fellow bishop, Lupus of Troyes and together they preached the true Apostolic Faith in many parts of the country, both in churches and outside in the streets and fields. Germanus with his legal background and lucid powers of reasoning was able to refute the heresy and to expound the orthodox teaching of the universal Church. The climax of his visit to Britain was reached when the two parties, with crowds of supporters on both sides, met together, possibly near the old Roman City of Verulamium, to debate the issue at stake. The bishops by their wise and eloquent speech were able to expose the weakness and falsity of the Pelagian position and Germanus won further support when he restored sight to a

---

*The Western Fathers. F. R. Hoare.

blind girl, a miracle which the Pelagians had declined to attempt.

After their spiritual victory the bishops visited the shrine of Alban, the martyr, to offer thanks to God and to add to it more relics. Before they returned to France Germanus with his military skill was able to help the Britons in a campaign against the Saxons who, according to a legendary accretion to the story, were put to rout by the battle cry of the British force. "Alleluia!" at which the terrified Saxons thought the sky and the rocks were falling upon them. Most of the British Christians remained loyal to the orthodox teaching of Germanus but a minority persisted in their error and in 446 he returned to Britain again, accompanied by Bishop Severus of Trier. They preached the Faith once more and finally banished the heretics from the country. Six or so churches in Wales are dedicated to Germanus for it was on the Welsh border that the Alleluia Victory reputedly took place. In England dedications number about twelve including the famous abbey at Selby in Yorkshire. In Norfolk the church of Wiggenhall St German is named in honour of the saint and in the north aisle a series of nineteenth century bench-ends depict scenes from his life. He appears also in the fifteenth century stained glass in the church of Wiggenhall St Mary Magdalene.

During the first half of the fifth century the British, under their chieftain Vortigern, invited Saxon mercenaries from the Continent to aid them in their struggle against the Picts in the north. In exchange for their military aid the Saxons were to be given payment, provisions and land in eastern Britain where they could settle and establish their base. Under this agreement the Saxon warriors crossed over to Britain in their three long ships, their leaders Hengist and Horsa. The traditional date of their arrival and that given by Bede is 449 but this cannot be fixed with absolute certainty. For this part of his *History* Bede bases his narrative on the writings of the British monk Gildas who was more of a moralist and theologian than an accurate historian.*

At first the Saxon mercenaries fulfilled their agreement with the British, defeated the Picts and restored peace to the island, but it soon became apparent that the Saxons were a treacherous ally intent on territorial gain for themselves. Like the Romans before them they saw that Britain was a rich land and worth conquering. To an agricultural people such as themselves, pressed by a shortage

---

De Excidio et Conquestu Britanniae. Gildas.

of land in their own continental homes, it must have seemed a country of great promise. Therefore they sent word to their homeland that the land was fertile, the Britons slack and cowardly and that more fighting men were needed. Soon reinforcements of Saxon warriors arrived in Britain, such hordes of them that the Britons began to live in terror of them for they were a pagan, uncultivated and war-like race. These warriors, too, were given land and provisions on condition that they maintained peace for the British, and this they did, making an alliance with the Picts. But the ultimate purpose of the Saxons was to conquer the land and a quarrel broke out between them and the British, deliberately provoked by the Saxons and intended to spark off trouble between the two peoples. The Saxons began to complain bitterly that their pay and food supplies were inadequate, threatening to devastate the whole country if they were not increased. Then they turned their weapons against those they had originally come to aid, killing thousands of them. The Anglo-Saxon Chronicle, which is an ancient record of events in Anglo-Saxon history, records that in the year 457 the Saxons under their leaders Hengist and his son Aesc killed four thousand Britons in the region of Kent, others fleeing to London for refuge.

The Britons who survived the massacre fled westwards to find refuge wherever they could, particularly in the mountainous regions of the west country; some left Britain and found refuge in Brittany; others surrendered to the Saxons and became absorbed into their society or served them as slaves. But when the remaining Britons had recovered from the onslaught they rallied under a new leader, Ambrosius Aurelianus and faced the heathen Saxons in renewed combat. A series of battles followed with victories gained on both sides, the most decisive for the British being fought in about AD 500 at the unidentified site of Badon Hill, a battle often associated with the military exploits of the legendary King Arthur. This battle was followed by a period of peace lasting some fifty years; but it was the Anglo-Saxons who were to achieve ultimate victory in the conflict and to gain complete mastery of the land by about the year 600.

Their conquest of Britain is thought to have been achieved in stages by separate bands of invaders, covering a period of almost two hundred years. There is no indication in the *Anglo-Saxon Chronicle* that it was achieved by a large and united invasion force such as had occurred in the time of the Roman conquest of Britain. We may imagine that droves of Saxon warriors crossed the

North Sea in their long, shallow, oar-propelled ships, similar to the late sixth century vessel found buried in the soil at Sutton Hoo in Suffolk which measured about eighty nine feet, with stations for forty oarsmen.* Their entry into Britain was chiefly by way of the east and south coasts, and the many river estuaries such as those of the Trent, the Nene, the Ouse, the Waveney, the Stour, the Thames and so on. Immigrants from their own homelands, their wives and families, flocked into the areas that had been conquered. They settled chiefly in the river valleys where the land was suitable for cultivation. With them the settlers brought their knowledge of agriculture and sheep and cattle rearing, their crafts and artistic skills, their music and minstrels, their poetry and songs, their love of war and feasting, their unwritten code of laws and their pagan gods, Woden, Thunor, Tiw and Frig.

Compared to the previous conquerors of Britain the English were an uncouth, illiterate and peasant race whose hearts were in the soil, the crops they produced and the animals they pastured. The fine stone buildings which the Romans had made appeared to them as "the work of giants" and for the most part they left them to ruin and built their own simple dwellings of clay and wattles and their larger timbered banqueting halls such as that excavated recently at Yeavering in Northumberland. In these halls they feasted and drank mead, told their tales of love and war and listened to the minstrels' songs, sung to the accompaniment of the harp. We must not think of these English settlers, however, merely as rough and untutored peasant folk with little achievement to their credit. The artefacts which have been unearthed from their graves reveal a high degree of artistic skill. Many of their brooches, buckles, swords and other metal objects, particularly those found among the Sutton Hoo treasure, are ornamented with beautiful and intricate designs which could only have been done by skilled workmen. These and other skills were developed more highly when the English had achieved a settled life and come under the influence of Continental Churchmen and Celtic missionaries.

As the invaders over a period of years conquered more and more of the land they settled in tribal regions each with its chieftain or king, though sometimes the government of a kingdom was shared by two or even three kings. In the early period of the settlement there were seven major kingdoms in England in

*The Sutton Hoo Ship Burial. R. Bruce-Mitford.

addition to several smaller kingdoms. The only kingdom north of the Humber was Northumbria, though this was sub-divided into Bernicia and Deira. The six remaining kingdoms of the Heptarchy that comprised southern England, were Mercia, Wessex, Kent, Sussex, Essex and East Anglia. Each was a separate, autonomous kingdom with its own royal house. Sometimes, if a particular king had become more powerful than other kings by his military victories, he would hold a position of authority over the other kingdoms and acquire the title of 'Bretwalda' or ruler of Britain.

Compared to Rome's highly organized and sophisticated system of government the organization and structure of Anglo-Saxon society was simple and primitive, but with clearly defined classes within its hierarchical framework. At the head of each tribal group was the king who claimed descent from the ancestral god, Woden, or in the case of Essex, from Saxnot. An advisory council known as the witan, composed of men of wisdom and discretion, was at hand to assist the king in the task of government, and to discuss with him the matters of state. Next in rank under the king came the noblemen among whom were the king's representatives or earldormen and his thanes. Below them were the commoners or freemen known as churls, the largest class in Anglo-Saxon society who were occupied in a variety of trades and professions, such as farming, sheep rearing, building, carpentry, and crafts of various kinds. At the bottom of the scale came the serfs who owned nothing and were employed by their masters to perform menial tasks. The Church was to exercise a strong influence in giving freedom to slaves; we find Bishop Wilfrid, for instance, freeing two hundred and fifty male and female slaves on the estate at Selsey in Sussex, given him by the king.* With the exception of slaves, each class of society had its appropriate worth in terms of money, its 'wergild' or price to be paid in compensation to a family for the murder of one of its members; if the wergild of a Kentish churl was a hundred shillings, this amount had to be paid to the man's kindred in the event of his being killed. Prescribed penalties were also laid down for other crimes and minor offences. The laws relating to early Anglo-Saxon society were at first unwritten but later under the influence of the Church they were committed to writing. We shall see later that St Augustine of Canterbury was responsible for encouraging King Ethelbert of Kent to write down the laws relating to his Kingdom.

*Bede. IV. 13.

The great missionary movement of the sixth and seventh centuries, led by St Augustine and his team of monks, took place against a background of paganism. The missionaries found the English practising the ancient religion of their Continental forefathers, with its own distinctive forms of worship and ritual, its priesthood, sacred shrines and temples and its pagan gods Tiw, Woden, Thunor and Frig which have given their names to our weekdays, Tuesday, Wednesday, Thursday, Friday, respectively, and also to numerous English place names. These gods were worshipped in sacred groves, forest clearings or on hill tops. At pagan festivals priests offered cakes and sacrificial beasts to the gods, chanting magical incantations and charms. Superstition and fear of demonic influences played a powerful role in shaping mens' behaviour; the world was haunted, or so it was believed, by hosts of supernatural creatures, ogres, elves and witches, whose malevolent influence could strike a man down with sickness or cause some other disaster to befall him. Against the power of such beings men recited charms, wore amulets or mixed strange potions. The *Penitential of Theodore,* the Archbishop of Canterbury from 668 to 690, reveals the extent to which early Anglo-Saxon society was dominated by superstition and a belief in witchcraft. Theodore prescribed seven years penance, three of them on bread and water, for those who attempted to cause the death of anyone by the practice of sorcery and seven years penance for a woman who tried to cure her daughter's sickness by putting her in the oven or on the roof, both being pagan practices. The Anglo-Saxon custom of burying the dead with their personal belongings, swords, shields, brooches, beads, girdle hangers, spindle whorls and so on, suggests a belief in survival after death. The custom has proved a valuable source of information to historians and archaeologists who have learnt much from these personal belongings which from time to time have been unearthed. The clearly defined Christian doctrine of personal salvation and life beyond the grave must have appeal d to a people already holding a vague belief in some kind of futu existence.

But when the missionaries first preached to the pagan king of Kent his reaction was cautious. "Your words and promises are fair indeed; but they are new and uncertain, and I cannot accept them and abandon the age-old beliefs that I have held together with the whole English nation."* The traditional beliefs, customs

---

*Bede. I. 25.

and superstitions of the Saxon people were deeply imbedded in their tribal life and were not easily relinquished in favour of a new and unfamiliar faith which propounded a God whom men could not even see. Only gradually did the new religion supplant the old. During the transition period faith fluctuated between paganism and Christianity. Men relapsed into paganism in times of crisis, attempting, for instance, to avert the plague by recourse to pagan practices. It is a common experience of Christian evangelists that new converts are reluctant to forsake certain of their heathen customs. These, if innocent, are sometimes retained or transformed by association with Christian ideas. Pope Gregory very wisely instructed his band of missionaries not to abolish all harmless customs nor to destroy pagan temples which could be converted to Christian use.

Anglo-Saxon kings exerted a strong influence over their people in religious, as in other, matters, giving a lead one way or another by their own acceptance or rejection of Christianity. When King Ethelbert of Kent finally accepted the new Faith, great numbers of his subjects did so too and came forward for baptism. But when his son and successor to the throne, King Eadbald, abandoned the Faith and practised abominable customs his subjects followed his lead and also reverted to idolatry. The apparent ease with which the people tended to revert to paganism in times of crisis and when their rulers did so, testifies to the shallowness of many of the early conversions to Christianity. The great weakness of the customary method of converting a kingdom from the king and his court downwards to the ordinary common folk was that conversion tended to be external and formal and lacking in spiritual depth, depending as Sir Arthur Bryant has said, "on the changing policies of a Court rather than on the hearts of a people."* However, even a formal acceptance of Christianity is not to be despised, for obedience to law often opens the way to the operation of grace, and there must have been, as there are in every age, many who understood the implications of the Faith and who advanced in the practise of it and guided others towards a clearer understanding of it.

We shall see in the chapters that follow that kings who had themselves accepted the new religion were often instrumental in effecting the conversion of other kings. We see it for example in

---

*The Story of England. Volume 1.

the relationship between King Oswy of Northumbria and King Sigbert of Essex. Sigbert, a pagan, frequently visited the court of his friend Oswy who had been converted to the Faith. Oswy reasoned with Sigbert and persuaded him that gods made of wood or stone, by man's handiwork were not gods at all but lifeless images. The true God, he said, whom the Christians worshipped, was of infinite majesty, almighty, creator, ruler and judge. After consulting with his advisory council Sigbert decided to abandon the old gods, to accept the Faith of Christ and to invite Christian teachers to his kingdom.

The failure of the Britons to preach the Faith to the pagan English is lamented by Bede but, he says, God sent them other more worthy preachers. These were to come from Rome as a result of a carefully planned campaign, inspired by Pope Gregory the Great, "who had a deep desire for the salvation of our people." The introduction of the Faith to pagan England and the subsequent activities of the Church were to have a widespread influence on the Anglo-Saxon settlers, substituting for their pagan religion, devoid as it was of moral and intellectual content and shrouded in superstition, one that was noble, rational and morally demanding. But the benefits brought by the Christians were not merely what one might narrowly term 'spiritual' for where Christianity is rightly practised and understood it irradiates every aspect of life, intellectual, moral, material and spiritual. Its introduction into Anglo-Saxon England was to prove an enriching and liberating experience to an illiterate, pagan and superstitious people.

One of the Church's major contributions towards their advancement was the dissemination among them of literacy and learning which was achieved mainly through the monastic schools. Bede, referring to the school at Canterbury where Theodore and Hadrian were the principal teachers, says, "Never had there been such happy times as these since the English settled in Britain. . . all who wished for instruction in the reading of the Scriptures found teachers ready at hand." The Church also encouraged the development of artistic skills, introducing to the English new forms of art and design which reached the height of their glory in the illuminated manuscripts which were made in the scriptoria of the monasteries.

To the high office of kingship the Church was to bring an enhanced significance, affirming that it was conferred upon men by divine appointment. The concept was well understood by the

Anglo-Saxons who already held a belief that their kings were descended from their ancestral gods. We shall see in the chapters that follow that throughout the conversion period there were close contacts between the clergy, God's representatives on earth, and the kings, appointed by God to rule. The conversion of a kingdom was only achieved so far as this rapport between clergy and rulers was maintained. No progress was made without the support of the royal families and in view of the close association that existed between them and the clergy it is not surprising that members of their families, princesses in particular, were so strongly influenced by the Christian missionaries. The seventh century saw the rise of a large number of double monasteries which provided for the training of both monks and nuns. In almost every case these monasteries were presided over by abbesses who were drawn from the royal families. Such abbesses were Etheldreda, from the royal house of East Anglia, who founded Ely monastery, and Hilda of Whitby, of the royal house of Northumbria, who founded Whitby abbey. It was the royal families who, in the first instance, experienced the full force of the missionaries' influence.

To these early monastic establishments we owe many of our cathedrals and churches of today. Though in most cases nothing remains of the original buildings, it was upon the sites of those foundations, or very close to them, that the ever more splendid buildings of successive generations were erected, thus maintaining a tradition of Christian worship which has survived over many centuries. Their origin dates back, in many cases, to the seventh century which saw a remarkable flowering of religious devotion in England and indeed of progress in every direction. Where today we have cathedrals such as Canterbury, Rochester, St Paul's, Ely and York, in the seventh century, on the same sites or thereabouts, were built smaller and simpler churches founded, with the assistance of secular rulers, by monks and nuns such as Augustine, Justus, Mellitus, Etheldreda, Paulinus and others, all of whom played a prominent role in spreading the Christian Faith among the pagan English. Although the Gospel was preached chiefly by men, women occupied an important place in Anglo-Saxon society and exercised a strong influence on the early English Church.

Our knowledge of the early saints of the English Church is derived largely from Bede's *Ecclesiastical History,* to which we have referred in the Introduction. In his Preface to the *History,* Bede tells his readers that he was encouraged to undertake the work by Albinus, abbot of the monastery of St Peter and St Paul in Canterbury. For much of his information about Augustine's mission to the people of Kent and the surrounding provinces Bede relied upon Albinus who studied the written records preserved at Canterbury. He conveyed the information to Bede, who was at work in the Northumbrian monastery of Monkwearmouth and Jarrow, through a priest of London, Nothelm, who both corresponded with Bede and went to his monastery to talk with him. Nothelm also visited Rome and with the pope's permission ferreted out relevant information about the English mission from the papal archives. He brought back letters of Pope Gregory which he passed on to Bede for inclusion in his *History*.

To present-day readers the characters who participated in the conversion of England thirteen centuries ago may seem shadowy and unreal. But we must remember that for Bede, the historian upon whom we are so dependent, many of them were almost his contemporaries. He was born in 672 or 673 which was about the time when Queen Etheldreda founded Ely minster. He was seven when she died in 680 and may very well have remembered, as a boy, hearing accounts of her life as Queen of Northumbria. Wilfrid, bishop of York, also gave him first hand information about Etheldreda, for the bishop was for many years chaplain and adviser to the queen. The characters, then, about whom Bede wrote, were not so far removed from his own time.

A second major source of information about this early period of English history is the *Anglo-Saxon Chronicle* which was compiled at the end of the ninth century. The oldest manuscript is the *Parker Chronicle*, so named because it once belonged to Matthew Parker, Archbishop of Canterbury from 1559 to 1575. It is now in the possession of Corpus Christi College, Cambridge. The entry in the *Chronicle* which will concern us in the next chapter is that for the year 596, an entry whose brevity is out of all proportion to its importance. It reads: "In this year Pope Gregory sent Augustine to Britian with very many monks who preached God's word to the English nation."*

In addition to the writings of Bede and the entries in the *Anglo-Saxon Chronicle* our knowledge of this early period of English history is derived from a diversity of sources: from a

---

The Anglo-Saxon Chronicle. Translated G. N. Garmonsway.

study of archaeological finds, from the evidence of place names and from various literary sources, charters, letters, legal codes, the *Lives of the Saints* and post-Conquest chronicles. References in extant works to other writings which have not survived indicate that a great deal more literary material once existed. Enough, however, has survived to give us a comprehensive picture of this fascinating period of our history when the English were emerging from the darkness of paganism into the light of Christian belief.

2 St Augustine's Mission to Kent

POPE Gregory the Great, the initiator of a scheme to convert the pagan English is often referred to as "the Apostle to the English" though his interest in our nation was but one item among a multiplicity of other papal concerns which demanded his attention. He was a man of shrewd and scholarly mind, practical common sense and deep piety. So great was his charity towards the poor of Rome that he distributed money, clothes and food to them and blamed himself when one destitute beggar died of starvation. He had been born and educated in Rome and at the age of thirty was made Prefect of the city with responsibility for its administration. At the height of his secular career and soon after the death of his father he surprised Rome by renouncing his inherited wealth, abandoning his career and converting his Roman villa into a monastery which he dedicated to St Andrew. At the same time he founded and endowed six monasteries in Sicily. He entered his own monastery in Rome as a simple monk and humbly placed himself under the direction of the man he had chosen to preside over it as abbot. Along with the other novices he learnt to observe the monastic rule based, it is thought, upon that of St Benedict.

It may have been during his novitiate at St Andrew's Monastery that Gregory encountered the fair-skinned English slave boys in Rome's market, so different from the swarthy Italian youths. When he enquired as to their place of origin he was told that they came from Britain and were heathens. "Alas!" said Gregory with a heart-felt sigh: "how sad that such bright-faced folk are still in the grasp of the author of darkness." When told that the boys belonged to the Angle race he replied, with a play upon the word, "That is appropriate, for they have angelic faces, and it is right that they should become joint-heirs with the angels in heaven"* But Gregory was distressed to know that the English lived in ignorance of the Christian Faith. Fired with missionary zeal he appealed to the pope, then Benedict I, to send preachers to Britain to convert

---

*Bede. II. 1.

34

the pagan English. He himself would go if the pope would grant him permission and, according to a *Life of Gregory*, written by a monk of Whitby, the pope did grant him permission and Gregory embarked upon his journey to Britain.* But the citizens of Rome, who had a great affection and respect for Gregory, protested so vigorously at this departure that the pope yielded to their entreaties and recalled him from the mission. At the same time Gregory received a sign from heaven "stay in this place." So he returned to Rome and the English people remained in heathen darkness.

When in 590 Gregory was himself elected to succeed Benedict I as pope he was able once more to direct his thoughts towards the conversion of the English. We find him in 595 writing a letter to Candidus, a priest, who was on his way to manage an estate in Gaul, asking him to use the money which he received from the estate to buy clothes for the poor and to redeem some English slave boys "that they may be given to God and educated in the monasteries."†
No doubt Gregory intended that the English boys should return later to their own land to preach the Gospel to their people. He had received news, most likely through the Christian queen of Kent, Bertha, and her chaplain Bishop Liudhard, that the English earnestly desired to have the Christian Faith preached to them. This news, reinforced by his own long-standing concern for their conversion led Pope Gregory to dispatch, in AD 596, a team of missionary monks led by Augustine to preach to the English nation.

Augustine had been praepositus, or prior, of Gregory's monastery of St Andrew in Rome and possessed the spiritual qualities and powers of leadership to fit him for the task of heading the mission. He was, too, a man of some learning having "a complete knowledge of the Scriptures." Though he himself played a major role in the enterprise we must not minimise the importance of the part played by his companions who, according to Bede, numbered about forty. Among these there must certainly have been men of outstanding intellectual, spiritual and practical ability, chosen not merely for their piety and missionary zeal but for the diversity of their gifts which would ensure the success of the mission. But

---

English Historical Documents. Volume 1. Number 152.

†*English Historical Documents*. Number 161.

whatever their personal gifts and qualities, all were dedicated to the service of God within a framework of monasticism, either as professed monks or as monks in training. By their vows of poverty, chastity and obedience they were free from the entanglements of worldly possessions, family ties and the enticements of self-will and so were able, after their preliminary setback, to pursue their purpose with single-minded devotion.

The party left Rome in 596, stayed with the bishop at Aix-en-Provence and at the island monastery of Lérins. At this juncture, and for a reason unknown, they were in doubt as to the wisdom of continuing their journey. Later Pope Gregory wrote to them urging them not to allow the tongues of evil-speaking men to deter them, so it is likely that their alarm had been caused by exaggerated tales of the savagery of the English race. Whatever the cause of their alarm they sent Augustine back to Rome with an appeal to the pope to recall them from "so dangerous, arduous, and uncertain a journey." But Gregory was not the sort of man to abandon an enterprise without good reason. Had he not cherished a desire to see the Faith of Christ preached to the English? He would not hear of recalling the missionaries; they must proceed and trust themselves to the protection of God. In his letter of encouragement and mild rebuke he shows himself to be a man of stern determination but also of deep kindliness.

Thus he wrote; "Gregory, Servant of the servants of God, to the servants of our Lord. My very dear sons, it is better never to undertake any high enterprise than to abandon it when once begun. So with the help of God you must carry out this holy task which you have begun. Do not be deterred by the troubles of the journey or by what men say. Be constant and zealous in carrying out this enterprise which, under God's guidance you have undertaken: and be assured that the greater the labour the greater will be the glory of your eternal reward. When Augustine, your leader, returns, whom we have appointed your abbot, obey him humbly in all things, remembering that whatever he directs you to do will always be to the good of your souls. May Almighty God protect you with his grace, and grant me to see the result of your labours in our heavenly home. And although my office prevents me from working at your side, yet because I long to do so, I hope to share in your joyful reward. God keep you safe, my dearest sons."*

*Bede. I. 23.

36

Augustine left Rome for the second time, carrying now this letter of encouragement from Pope Gregory to show to his fellow monks when he joined them again in Gaul. In addition, Gregory gave Augustine other letters of commendation and gifts to be delivered to bishops and secular rulers through whose territory the monks would travel. Heartened by the words of Pope Gregory the monks made their way northwards through Gaul, using wherever possible the old Roman roads, lodging in monasteries or with clergy and presenting their letters of commendation, until they reached a port in northern Gaul, probably Quentavic (Étaples). From here, accompanied by interpreters, the monks sailed for Britain. If Augustine had left a record of his Channel crossing and his landing at Ebbsfleet in Kent it might have made as interesting reading as Julius Caesar's record of the same voyage some centuries earlier when his legions looked towards the white cliffs of Dover and saw on those heights the enemy ranks arrayed for battle. But Caesar had come to Britain equipped for war, intent on subduing the land and her people; Augustine had come with a message of peace, intent only on subduing the pagan souls of the English to the easy yoke of Christ.

England at the time of Augustine's arrival in 597 was divided, as we have seen, into a number of separate kingdoms each with its own king, one of whom held the title of Bretwalda. Ethelbert, king of Kent, held this position when the missionaries from Rome landed in his kingdom and announced their desire to preach to his people. Bede describes Ethelbert as a powerful monarch exercising authority over lands as far north as the Humber, the natural boundary between the southern and northern English. The missionaries, then, were to begin their preaching from Kent, the most influential and perhaps the most thickly populated of the kingdoms south of the Humber. Its close proximity to Gaul exposed it to cultural and religious influences from the Continent and offered it greater trading opportunities than existed for other kingdoms, apart, perhaps, from East Anglia which also shows signs, in the discoveries made in the excavation of burial sities, of a material prosperity similar to that of Kent. Julius Caesar, who landed in Kent in 55BC and again in 54BC had said of this part of Britain, "Of all the Britons the inhabitants of Kent, an entirely maritime district, are by far the most civilized, differing but little from the Gallic manner of life."* This was still true of Kent six

---

*The Gallic War. V. 14. Translated H. J. Edwards.

centuries later when the district was populated by the Anglo-Saxon settlers. The close tie between Kent and Gaul was further strengthened by a marriage alliance between the two royal families. In 560 Ethelbert, the young king of Kent, married the Princess Bertha, daughter of Charibert, king of Paris. Ethelbert was a pagan worshipper of Thunor and Woden, and remained so until the arrival of the missionaries from Rome in 597. Bertha was a Christian and was given in marriage by her parents on condition that she should be allowed to practise her own religion rather than adopt that of her husband. She brought to England her own chaplain, Bishop Liudhard, and was given, for her religious devotions, the small chapel of St Martin on the east side of Canterbury. Here she worshipped God for a number of years before she saw the conversion of her husband and people.

Augustine's momentous landing in Britain took place on Thanet island which was separated from the Kentish mainland by the Wantsum Channel, or the river Stour, as we know it. His first concern was to secure the interest and support of King Ethelbert and to gain his permission to preach in Kent. We have referred in Chapter 1 to the close association that existed, during the conversion period, between religious and secular rulers. For the most part this association was mutually advantageous and amicable. Royal backing for the missionaries ensured them freedom to preach throughout the kingdom and if the king himself decided to embrace the new Faith half the battle was won against paganism, for his subjects would follow his lead. But the missionaries received more than spiritual support from the royal families; it was from them that they received grants of land on which to build their churches and monasteries. The pages of Bede contain many references to such endowments and to the gifts which the monks received from royal persons. The missionaries in turn brought to the royal houses the benefits of their culture and learning, their wisdom and counsel and above all a new religion which enhanced the office of kingship, investing it with divine authority.

Augustine and his fellow monks from Rome knew nothing of the Anglo-Saxon language when they arrived in Kent, though we may assume that they gained a knowledge of it later. Before crossing the Channel they had recruited men in Gaul, who had a knowledge of the Kentish dialect, to act as interpreters. These men were sent to the royal city of Canterbury to inform King

Ethelbert of Augustine's arrival from Rome and to tell him the purpose of their mission. Ethelbert invited them to stay on the island until he had decided what should be done about them and he ordered that food and other necessities should be given them. After several days Ethelbert and his retainers came to Thanet to meet Augustine and his companions and to hear their message. The encounter took place in the open and must have been a memorable one. The monks advanced in procession towards the king, carrying a silver cross and a wooden banner on which was painted a representation of Christ. They sang litanies and prayed for the salvation of the people to whom they had come. Then the king commanded them to sit down and to tell him about the faith which they desired to preach to his people. With the help of interpreters Augustine and his fellow monks preached the Word of Life to the royal assembly. King Ethelbert was moved by the graciousness of their message but replied that he could not forsake his own traditional beliefs which he shared with the whole English race. He knew that they had travelled far for the purpose of spreading their beliefs to his people and he did not forbid them to do this. He assured them that no harm would come to them and invited them to live in his own city of Canterbury, providing them with a residence of their own and giving them permission to use the church of St Martin where hitherto Queen Bertha had worshipped the Christian God.

Bede gives an account of the daily life of these early missionaries. It was regulated according to the pattern of the Apostolic Church. They prayed, fasted and kept vigils, despised worldly possessions, endured hardships and held their Faith with such devotion that they were willing to die for it. They preached the Gospel to the heathen, setting them a good example by the innocence and simplicity of their own lives. Soon the pagan English began to feel the influence of these holy men among them and many declared their belief in the true God, desiring to be baptized. The church of St Martin was used for public worship, for celebrations of the Eucharist, for prayer, preaching, the singing of psalms and for the baptism of new converts, though it is likely that some baptisms also took place in the open air when the weather was favourable. We know from Bede that in Northumbria Bishop Paulinus baptized new converts in the river Glen at Yeavering, in the Trent at Littleborough and in the Swale at Catterick.

According to a Canterbury tradition King Ethelbert's baptism took place on Whitsunday, 2nd June 597 in the church of St Martin. Tradition has connected his baptism with the ancient font now in St Martin's Church and modern artists in stained glass have copied this font in their depictions of the baptism. But archaeologists believe it to be of a much later date than the sixth century.* It is more likely that the king was baptized in a font similar to the leaden tanks inscribed with the Chi-Rho and Alpha-Omega monograms which were used by Christians in late Roman and early Anglo-Saxon times. But whatever the mode of the baptism the occasion was an important one, for Ethelbert was the first English king to become a Christian. How meaningful the ceremony would have been to him, we cannot tell. He was a power-ful ruler and had gained his ascendancy over other kingdoms by his military strength. His faith until now had been in the pagan gods, Thunor and Woden. Perhaps he never quite lost his faith in them. Was it not due to their favour and protection that he had gained his victories? Could he not maintain his hold on them and in addition give his allegiance to the new God of the Christians? But the whole tenor of Bede's narrative suggests that Ethelbert's conversion was sincere and genuine and that he had a clear understanding of the meaning of the Faith. Having accepted it himself he began to encourage its advance in his kingdom and rejoiced when his subjects turned from paganism to belief in Christ. But he compelled no one, for he had learned from the Christian teachers that "the service of Christ must be accepted freely and not under compulsion." Ethelbert also made many gifts to the missionaries and gave them a more permanent and suitable dwelling in Canterbury.

Pope Gregory wrote to Ethelbert, exhorting him to encourage the spread of Christianity in his kingdom, ". . .Therefore, my illustrious son, zealously foster the grace that God has given you, and press on with the task of extending the Christian Faith among the people committed to your charge. Make their conversion your first concern; suppress the worship of idols, and destroy their shrines; raise the moral standards of your subjects by your own innocence of life. . ." Let the king, he continued, be like the great Emperor Constantine whose own conversion to the Faith was the means of turning the Roman Empire from idolatrous worship to the worship of Jesus Christ. Let the king also take heed, said Gregory,

---

*St Martin's Church, Canterbury. C. F. Routledge.

to the advice of Bishop Augustine — he had been consecrated bishop by the time this letter was written — for Augustine was a man of holy life, trained in monastic discipline and possessing a wide knowledge of the Scriptures. Pope Gregory also wished the king to know that the end of the world was surely approaching; the signs preceding the end were sent to warn us to prepare our souls to meet our Judge.

A second letter, written by Pope Gregory, is of interest in connection with the conversion of the English nation. It was addressed to Eulogius, bishop of Alexandria and dated July 598. Gregory tells Eulogius of the plans he had made to send missionaries to England and of the subsequent success of the mission. "While the people of the English," he says, "placed in a corner of the world, remained until now in the false worship of stocks and stones, I resolved, with the aid of your prayers, to send by God's instigation a monk of my monastery to preach to that people. . . And even now letters have reached us telling of his safety, and of his work, that both he and those that were sent with him shine amongst that race with such miracles that the miracles of the Apostles seem to be imitated in the signs which they exhibit. And on the feast of our Lord's Nativity. . . more than ten thousand of the English are reported to have been baptized by this our brother and fellow-bishop."*

*English Historical Documents. Volume I. Number 163.

3   Further Developments in Kent

IN A letter to Queen Brunhild of the Franks, written in September 597, Pope Gregory refers to Augustine as "our brother and fellow bishop". Bede states that he was consecrated archbishop of the English at Arles in southern France, presumably by Vergilius who was at that time archbishop of Arles, and not by Etherius as Bede says.* He returned to Britain as the first archbishop of Canterbury possessing now the authority to bestow episcopal and priestly ordination on his fellow monks and any others who were sent to join his mission to the English. By this means the expansion of the Christian Church was ensured both within Kent itself and outside it. By 604 we find that Augustine had consecrated bishops to serve at Rochester and at London as well as consecrating Laurence to succeed him as archbishop of Canterbury.

On his return to Britain Augustine sent two of his companions, Laurence the priest and Peter the monk, to Rome to report to Pope Gregory on the progress of the mission and to submit to him a number of queries on church discipline and matters of moral concern to the English, "these uncouth English people require guidance on all these matters," said Augustine. He appealed also to the pope to send him more helpers. It is evident that few of the monks who had originally come to Britain with Augustine possessed the necessary qualifications for important positions of leadership and responsibility in the young English Church and it was for such positions that Augustine needed more helpers. Among the second band of monks sent by the pope in 601 Augustine was able to promote two, Justus and Mellitus, to bishoprics, and a third, Paulinus, was later consecrated bishop, and sent to preach the Faith in Northumbria. With this second group of monks the pope sent great quantities of ecclesiastical equipment and the pallium for Augustine, which was a vestment to be worn on solemn occasions as a sign of his office; he sent also "sacred vessels, altar coverings, church ornaments, vestments for priests and clergy, relics of the holy Apostles and martyrs, and many books." One of the

---

*See note, Bede. I. 27. Colgrave and Mynors.

treasures of Corpus Christi College Cambridge is a Latin Gospel book, written and illuminated in a sixth century Italian hand and according to a Canterbury tradition associated with Augustine himself; it may possibly have been brought by him from Rome or have been among the many books sent to him in 601 by Pope Gregory. It is certain that Augustine and his companions would have had special need for copies of the Scriptures, the Gospels in particular. Other books used by the preachers would have included copies of the Psalter, Latin chants, Service books and Litanies and there is little doubt that they would have possessed and made constant use of Pope Gregory's own manual for bishops and priests known as *Pastoral Care.* Later, when English boys were recruited and trained in St Augustine's and other monasteries a wide range of books would have been needed for their education, including Jerome's Latin version of the Scriptures, commentaries, *Saint's Lives,* writings of the early Fathers, historical works, monastic rules and so on.

St Augustine received instructions from Pope Gregory that the pagan idols of the English were to be destroyed but their temples, if in a serviceable condition, were to be sprinkled with holy water, purged of all corrupt associations and dedicated to the service of God; the preservation of their own buildings would encourage the English to continue to use them and so they would be led gently to the abandonment of idolatry and to an acceptance of the true Faith. The slaughter of oxen was also to be allowed to continue but not for the sake of offering them to pagan gods; the animals were to be killed and eaten by the people at some Christian festival and thanks to be given to God for his bounty. By allowing these outward enjoyments to continue, said Gregory, the people would "more readily come to desire the joys of the spirit. For it is certainly impossible to eradicate all errors from obstinate minds at one stroke, and whoever wishes to climb to a mountain top climbs gradually step by step, and not in one leap."

By the beginning of the seventh century the Christian Church had become firmly established in Kent. The king and many thousands of his subjects had forsaken their heathen customs and received Christian baptism. Never before had they heard such teaching or witnessed such miracles as those which Augustine performed; when he prayed earnestly to his God and laid his hands on the sick they recovered. News of his wonder-working powers reached Pope Gregory who thought it necessary to write to him to warn him lest this spiritual grace which was so wonderfully displayed in him, should engender pride in his soul. He must be thankful that the conversion of the English was being forwarded by their witness of these miracles, but he must beware lest his own power to perform them led to conceit. Let the memory of his own sins keep him humble and let him remember that any power he had received from God to work miracles was entirely for the benefit of those whom he had come to convert.

Since Augustine's landing in Britain in 597 Canterbury had become the nerve-centre of Christianity in south east England. The pope had intended London to be the seat of the first archbishop of the English people, but after gaining the support of King Ethelbert of Kent it was of paramount importance for Augustine to maintain this friendship with a king who at that time, as Bretwalda, had great influence over all the kingdoms of the southern English. London was not within Kentish territory but was in Essex which was governed by Ethelbert's nephew Sabert. But we shall see later that Ethelbert exercised his influence over Sabert in the matter of his conversion.

Augustine foresaw that if Canterbury was to remain the centre of Church life in England additional buildings and churches were essential. A house fit for himself and his family of clergy and lay brothers was needed, which in future would be occupied by the archbishops who would succeed him. Above all a monastery must be built where the monks, who had come with him from Rome, together with recruits from among the English, could live out their Christian Faith under the discipline of monastic vows. Augustine's plans for the future of the Church in Canterbury had first to receive the approval and support of the King and this Ethelbert gladly gave. He allowed Augustine to restore a church in Canterbury built originally in Roman times, which he dedicated to Christ our Saviour and where today on the same site stands Canterbury cathedral. King Ethelbert also granted Augustine land to the east of the city for the founding of a monastery, vestiges of which still remain. The monastery and its nearby church were dedicated to the Apostles St Peter and St Paul but in the tenth century it became known as St Augustine's Abbey in honour of the saint who brought the Faith to England. The church, which was not completed or dedicated until after Augustine's death, was richly endowed by King Ethelbert, for not only was it to serve as a monastic church but it was also to become the last resting place for secular and ecclesiastical rulers. Here in the church of St Peter and St Paul, in the porticus on the north side of the nave, the body of Augustine was later to be laid to rest and in the porticus to the south of the nave were to lie the bodies of King Ethelbert and Queen Bertha.

To an illiterate people such as the pagan English, education was an important feature of the Christian mission. We know that by about the year 630 a school existed at Canterbury, for Bede tells us that when King Sigbert and Bishop Felix of East Anglia wished to establish a school in their kingdom they obtained teachers and masters from the school in Canterbury, attached we may assume, to the monastery of St Peter and St Paul. Bede makes no mention of the founding of a school in Canterbury by Augustine, but it is likely that this Canterbury school to which he refers in connection with East Anglia was in fact founded by him or by members of his team of helpers. We shall see that by the end of the seventh century in the time of Archbishop Theodore, the monastery of St Peter and St Paul had become a centre of learning, attracting large numbers of distinguished pupils. But in the early stages of the mission it is likely too that schools were established to teach and train English boys who aspired to serve the Church as priests, deacons, monks or lay-brothers. It was certainly the policy of the missionaries from Rome to train native clergy to work among their own people; we read in Bede's *History* of a number of English bishops at work in the second half of the seventh century: Ithamar of Kent who became bishop of Rochester, Bertgils from Kent and Thomas from the Fens, both becoming bishops of East Anglia.

The education which the boys received in these early schools in Kent and elsewhere would have included subjects which had a direct bearing on the Christian Faith and the Church Services. The curriculum would have comprised reading and writing, Latin, music and a knowledge of the Gregorian Chant, a study of the Scriptures with commentaries and methods of calculating the Easter Festival. Some boys would have been taught the art of copying the Scriptures and other works on to vellum and illuminating them with colourful designs. The absence of secular studies at this early stage of the conversion was most likely due to the missionaries' pre-occupation with the primary purpose of their mission, which was to convert the heathen and to instruct them in the Faith of Christ. The untutored English would not have required, at this stage, instruction in Greek, Classical Literature, Law or

Rhetoric and in any case Augustine was under the pope's authority and Gregory would not have permitted the dissemination of secular knowledge to the pagan English. "Holy Scripture," said Gregory, "is incomparably superior to every form of knowledge and science. It preaches the truth and calls us to our heavenly Fatherland."* In a letter to Desiderius, bishop of Vienne, Gregory reproved him for advancing the study of Classical Literature. "Please do consider, how unutterably wicked it is for a bishop to declaim aloud lines of poetry not even meet for a devout layman. . ."†

We have referred, in Chapter 1, to the unwritten code of laws which the Anglo-Saxons brought with them to Britain. These were their own traditional Germanic folk-laws. It was not until the coming of Augustine and the introduction into their society of Christianity, a religion with a deep respect for law, that these laws, or a selection of them, were put into writing. Ethelbert, with the help of his counsellors and Bishop Augustine, collected and wrote down this earliest code of Kentish laws, formulated most likely in (AD 602-3.‡ They are of particular interest as being the first known document to be written in the vernacular language, Anglo-Saxon or English. In addition to their own Germanic laws, others were included which safeguarded the Church, its clergy, its property and its place in society. The code, which comprised 90 laws, opens as follows:

These are the decrees which King Aethelberht established in the life time of Augustine.

(1) (the theft of) God's property and the Church's shall be compensated twelve fold; a bishop's property elevenfold; a priest's property ninefold; a deacon's property sixfold; a clerk's property threefold. Breach of the peace shall be compensated doubly when it affects a church or a meeting place.

Then follow laws which ensure the safety of the king, his servants and property:

(2) If a king calls his lieges to him and anyone molests them there, he shall pay double compensation and 50 shillings to the king.

---

*The Gregorian Mission and English Education. P. F. Jones, Speculum, 1928.

† The Gateway to the Middle Ages. Chapter IV. E. S. Duckett.

‡ The Laws of the Earliest English Kings. F. L. Attenborough.

The remainder of the code concerns laws relating to various offences such as murder, for which a compensation was imposed according to the social status of the victim, laws regarding theft and highway robbery, sexual offences and injury to a man's person or property, wife or servants.

(27)   If a freeman breaks the fence round (another man's) enclosure he is to pay 6 shillings compensation.

(69)   If a foot is struck off 50 shilling shall be paid for it.

(70)   If a big toe is struck off 10 shillings shall be paid for it.

(82)   If a man forcibly carries off a maiden (he shall pay) 50 shillings to her owner. . .*

No account of Augustine's mission in Britain would be complete without some mention of his attempt, fruitless though it was, to win the allegiance and co-operation of the Celtic, or British clergy who worked among their own people, chiefly in the northern and western areas of Britain. It will be remembered that the Romano-British people had struggled to stave off the Anglo-Saxon invaders, but they had failed to do so and had been driven westwards and northwards to the hill country where they were safe from the invaders. The Christians among them had been little influenced as yet by the missionaries from Rome and they had retained their distinctive form of Christianity, which though not doctrinally heretical, was out of line with certain Roman customs and practices. The concern which the Roman Church felt towards the Celtic Christians ostensibly hinged upon the Celtic refusal to adopt the Roman method of calculating the date of Easter, which could sometimes result in their celebrating the feast a week earlier than the Roman Christians, secondly upon their refusal to administer baptism according to Roman rites and thirdly upon their refusal to adopt the Roman form of tonsure.† But underlying these ritual divergences Rome's real concern was for the unity of Christendom. Pope Gregory had made Augustine's position clear from the start, "All the bishops of Britain, we commit to your charge. Use your authority to instruct the unlearned, to strengthen the weak, and correct the misguided." At a | conference held at St Augustine's Oak on the border of

---

*The Laws of the Earliest English Kings. F. L. Attenborough.

†For a discussion of these divergences see *Venerabilis Baedae*, Latin Text and Notes, page 348. C. Plummer.

Wessex, Augustine's first attempt to establish brotherly relations with the Celtic Church in western Britain and to persuade their clergy to aid him in the task of preaching the Faith to the pagan English, failed to move them from their intransigent position, for they "stubbornly preferred their own customs to those in universal use among Christian Churches." A second conference, attended by seven British bishops and many learned monks from Bangor monastery in Wales was equally fruitless. Augustine failed to rise from his seat when the British bishops approached, a sign, they thought, of a lack of Christian courtesy and meekness. They refused to accept his three proposals: to keep Easter according to Roman reckoning, to follow the Roman rites of baptism and to join him in preaching to the English. With regard to the latter proposal, were not the heathen English the enemies of the British and had they not driven them from their homes, conquered their lands and enslaved thousands of their people? How then could Augustine expect them to offer the hand of friendship to these heathen barbarians? Neither Augustine nor his successor Laurence who, "sought to extend his pastoral care to the original inhabitants of Britain" made any effective progress in gaining the submission of the Celtic Church to the authority of Rome. Only gradually did this occur after the Synod of Whitby in AD 664 when it was agreed that Roman practices should be obeyed by the entire Church.

Among the second group of monks whom Pope Gregory had sent in 601 to help Augustine we have seen that there were some able and suited to be leaders of men. After working for three years with Augustine in Kent they had gained an insight into the Anglo-Saxon character, a knowledge of their language and experience of preaching the Christian Faith to a heathen race. In 604 Augustine consecrated two of these fellow workers to bishoprics: Justus to Rochester in western Kent, where Ethelbert founded a cathedral church and dedicated it to St Andrew, a dedication which survives to this day in Rochester Cathedral; and Mellitus to London, the capital of the kingdom of the East Saxons, or Essex as we know it. Ethelbert encouraged its king, Sabert, to receive Christian baptism and in the royal city of London he founded a church dedicated to St Paul.

Not long after making these ecclesiastical appointments and consecrating Laurence to be his successor as archbishop of Canterbury, Augustine, "a man beloved of God" died in 604 or

605. His body was laid to rest outside the monastic church of St Peter and St Paul which was still in the process of construction, but immediately it was finished his body was buried in the northern porticus of the church, his tomb bearing the epitaph:

Here rests the Lord Augustine, first Archbishop of Canterbury, who, having been sent here by blessed Gregory, Pontiff of the City of Rome, and supported by God with miracles, guided King Ethelbert and his people from the worship of idols to the Faith of Christ. . .*

After a reign of over fifty years King Ethelbert died in 616 and was buried beside his wife Bertha in the south porticus of the church of St Peter and St Paul. He had married again after the death of Bertha and he left a young widow whom his son Eadbald subsequently married, thereby incurring the disapproval of the Church. Pope Gregory in response to Augustine's queries on the subject of marriage with one's kindred had said "to wed one's step-mother is a grave sin." But such marriages were not uncommon among the Anglo-Saxon people on the Continent before their conversion to Christianity. Bede tells us that the Church in Kent suffered a setback when Eadbald came to the throne for he rejected the Faith and encouraged a reversion to idolatry. So deeply disheartened was Archbishop Laurence that he thought it wise to abandon the mission and to return to Rome. Mellitus, bishop of the East Saxons had already been expelled from London by the three reigning kings and he and Justus had returned to Gaul. Laurence planned to follow them but was deflected from his purpose by a vision of the Apostle Peter who reproached him for wishing to desert his flock. Laurence subsequently repented of his decision and went to King Eadbald to relate his vision which so amazed and awed the king that he decided to accept the Christian Faith, to marry according to the Church's law and to foster the spread of Christianity in his kingdom.

From the time of King Eadbald's conversion and the subsequent recovery of the Church a number of monasteries were founded in Kent which were to play a vital role in the spread of the Faith in that kingdom. The king made grants of land to both his sister and his daughter for the foundation of monasteries, or minsters, as they are better known. His sister Ethelberga, daughter of King Ethelbert, had left her native Kent to become the wife of

---

*Bede. II. 3.

49

Northumbria's king, Edwin, who in the early years of their marriage was not a Christian but later became so. The Princess took with her to Northumbria a chaplain, Paulinus, a member of the second group of missionaries sent by Gregory from Rome in 601. Eight years after Ethelberga's marriage her husband was killed in battle against Cadwallon of North Wales and his ally Penda of Mercia. After her husband's death in 633 she returned with her chaplain and attendants to Kent where her brother Eadbald was king. Ethelberga wished to devote the rest of her life to the service of God under the vows of religion and for this purpose Eadbald gave her land and property at Lyminge in southern Kent for the foundation of a double minster for nuns and monks. The present church at Lyminge is believed by archaeologists to contain vestiges of the original seventh century building which would have been like other Kentish churches of this period, a small simple building copied from the Italian style with a rectangular nave and triple arches separating it from the semi-circular apse.*

Ethelberga's double minster was typical of a number of such religious houses founded in the seventh century providing religious training for both men and women. Professor Knowles in *The Christian Centuries* says that they took the form of "a large nunnery ruled by an abbess of royal or noble blood with a group of monks attached, who, besides acting as chaplains to the nuns, ministered to the surrounding population. All were under the rule of the abbess, and some of these, notably Hilda of Whitby, Etheldreda of Ely, and Milburg of Wenlock were women of great ability and sanctity, who helped to diffuse learning as well as religion." There was of course complete segregation of the sexes except for services in the church, though at Wimborne the monks and nuns worshipped in separate churches.

A second minster founded in Kent by King Eadbald was for his daughter Eanswyth at Folkestone, built on the cliff top, not far from the present church of St Mary and St Eanswyth. It was probably the earliest of the Kentish minsters and founded in about AD 630. According to tradition Eanswyth served her novitiate in north west Gaul where double monasteries were at that time common. Then she returned to Kent and became abbess of the minster at Folcaston (Folkestone). The present church founded

*For seventh century churches see *The Pre-Conquest Church in England*. Margaret Deanesley.

in 1138 claims to possess some relics of the saint for in 1885, when alterations were being made to the north wall, a Saxon casket of lead was discovered and in it were some bones which archaeologists of the time declared to be those of a young woman. The alleged relics now rest in a shrine in the north wall of the chancel.

The Isle of Sheppey was the site of another of these Kentish minsters. It was built on the north of the island by Sexburg the wife of King Earconbert (640-664) who succeeded Eadbald. He is chiefly remembered for his firm policy regarding the destruction of idols and heathen shrines, a policy enforced by law with penalties for the disobedient. Sexburg was a devout Christian and the daughter of King Anna of East Anglia. When Sexburg's husband died of plague in 664 she acted as regent for her young son Egbert until he was old enough to reign. Then, on land given her by Egbert, she founded the minster in Sheppey, received the veil from Archbishop Theodore and for some years ruled the minster as its first abbess. But her real desire was to live quietly as a simple nun. Where better could she find than her sister Etheldreda's double monastery in the peaceful, fenland district of Ely? Handing over the minster in Sheppey to her daughter, Ermenilda, she retired to Ely where later she was to become abbess. But the minster she had founded at Sheppey became a centre of Christian witness on the island for almost two hundred years until in the ninth century it was plundered and destroyed by the Danes. Today on the same magnificent site stands the fine old parish church, dedicated to St Mary and St Sexburg, its north wall almost certainly part of the original seventh century minster church.

King Egbert is also the reputed founder of a minster in Thanet; he gave land to his cousin Domneva, the first abbess who was succeeded by her more illustrious daughter Mildred, a popular Anglo-Saxon saint to whom many churches were dedicated. But more is known of the minster's third abbess, Eadburg, a gifted and learned woman who brought great fame to the minster. She evidently encouraged the art of copying and illuminating manuscripts at Thanet and may have been accomplished in the art herself. Boniface, missionary to the Germans, with whom she corresponded for many years asked her for a copy of the Epistles of St Peter, "write for me in letters of gold the Epistles of my Lord St Peter the Apostle, to secure honour and reverence for

Holy Scriptures when they are preached before the eyes of the heathen. . ."*

A religious house for monks at Reculver was, according to the *Anglo-Saxon Chronicle,* founded in 669 by Egbert; the entry reads "King Egbert gave Reculver to Bass the priest to build a church there." Bede tells us that one of the abbots of this monastery was Bertwald who was "learned in the Scriptures and well versed in ecclesiastical and monastic affairs." Later he was to become archbishop of Canterbury. Reculver, as we have seen, was the site of one of the Saxon Shore forts and guarded the northern entrance to the Wansum Channel. The seventh century church was built in the centre of the ruined fortress area, incorporating in its structure quantities of Roman bricks and masonry. Remains of this ancient church were discovered in 1926.

Visitors to the sites of these Kentish minsters and to others outside Kent cannot fail to be impressed by their excellent geographical position with their commanding views of sea and landscape: St Ethelberga's at Lyminge set in a panorama of attractive countryside, St Eanswyth's at Folkestone overlooking the English Channel, St Sexburgh's at Sheppey with splendid views of the Swale and the Kentish hills on the one side and the estuaries of the Thames and Medway on the other, and Reculver on the north Kent coast. The choice of these sites and others at Ely, Whitby, and Coldingham was no doubt conditioned by the availability of royal estates, for all were founded by grants from the royal families. Other practical considerations had to be taken into account, such as their proximity to ports and serviceable roads, the availability of building materials and water supply. But we may conjecture that their founders also had an eye to the beauty of the sites and their suitability as dwelling places for men and women devoted to a life of prayer and study.

From minsters such as these, whether single or twin establishments, the conversion of England was achieved. Their expansion was promoted and encouraged by men of the Roman or Celtic church who were themselves monks. In the second half of the seventh century we find in particular, Archbishop Theodore encouraging the growth of monasticism in England. He himself had spent many years in a monastery in Rome before becoming archbishop of Canterbury.

---

*English Historical Documents. Volume I. Number 172.

Of the seventh century archbishops who succeeded Augustine, Theodore was the most celebrated, being both scholarly and statesmanlike. Augustine's work at the beginning of the century had been chiefly confined to Kent but by the end of the century the Faith had spread to all the English kingdoms and it was the task of Theodore to consolidate the work of Augustine and his successors and to give shape and unity to the Church. Bede describes him as "the first archbishop whom the entire Church in England obeyed." He was born in Tarsus in Cilicia, educated in the classical tradition at Athens and Rome and was a monk in that city when at the age of sixty-six his name was put forward to the pope as a likely candidate for the archbishopric of Canterbury. The pope had wished to consecrate Hadrian, an abbot of a monastery near Naples, but Hadrian had declined so high an office and recommended Theodore instead. Theodore was consecrated in Rome in 668 and was archbishop until his death in 690. He travelled to England with Hadrian who had been instructed by the pope to support the new archbishop in his work and to ensure that none of the customs of the Greek Church were introduced into England. Both men were scholars and under their influence the monastery of St Peter and St Paul at Canterbury reached the height of its fame, attracting pupils like Albinus who gave such great assistance to Bede in the writing of his *History*, Tobias, a scholar of Latin, Greek and Saxon who was to become bishop of Rochester, and the great scholar of Malmesbury, Aldhelm, later bishop of Sherborne.

Soon after his arrival in England in 669 Theodore accompanied by Hadrian made a visitation on foot and on horseback of all the areas of England, including Northumbria, where churches had been established — a strenuous undertaking for a man of Theodore's age. Everywhere he corrected abuses in the churches, teaching the right way of Christian living and urging the correct observance of Easter. He consecrated men to bishoprics wherever they were needed because their numbers had fallen since the severe outbreak of plague in 664; Putta was appointed to Rochester, Chad to Lichfield and Wilfrid was restored to York after having been expelled by King Egfrid.

Theodore introduced into the Church of England the practice of holding annual synods at which bishops and other religious leaders and teachers discussed the business of the Church. The first of the synods was held at Hertford in 672 with the names of the delegates, the business discussed and the decisions passed, recorded by the synod's secretary, Titillus. Among the matters discussed was the need for existing bishoprics to be divided and more bishops to be consecrated, a need which arose from the rapid growth of the Church. The proposal was unpopular among some bishops, Wilfrid of York in particular, though he was not present at the Conference and sent representatives from his diocese; but Theodore clearly intended to follow the proposed policy and not long after the synod he divided the very large East Anglian see, followed in 678 by the division of Northumbria. It was in matters such as these, in the field of organization and administration that Theodore made his major contribution to the Church of England. But he is remembered too for his promotion of learning at the Canterbury schools which drew students from England, Ireland and the Continent, and for his *Penitential,* which was a collection of his judgements on matters of morality, heresy and heathen practices compiled by his disciples after his death. It formed an ethical framework for the teaching of the newly converted English people and influenced the Church of western Europe for centuries to come.

4 St Felix—Apostle of East Anglia

APART from sending Mellitus to London to preach to the East Saxons Augustine made no attempt, as far as we know, to evangelize any of the English kingdoms outside Kent. He was archbishop of Canterbury for only seven or eight years and concentrated all his efforts on the conversion of Kent and the establishment of the metropolitan see at Canterbury, and when Bishop Felix came from Burgundy in 630 wishing to work among the heathen English it was from Canterbury that he received his authority to preach the Faith in East Anglia.

Our information about the early Church in East Anglia is derived chiefly from Bede who, in his *History,* states that his knowledge of the province, its conversion, its kings and bishops, is drawn from old writings and traditions, from the accounts of Abbot Esi and from Albinus, abbot of the monasteries of St Peter and St Paul, Canterbury, a reliable scholar trained under Hadrian and Theodore. Our dependence upon Bede is all the greater because of the absence of other sources of information regarding East Anglia, such as charters and letters. Bede includes in his *History,* accounts of the work of Felix, Fursey and Etheldreda of Ely. Many legends have arisen in connection with these, and other, saints which the reader should guard against accepting as historical fact. In a recent article entitled *The Pre-Viking Age Church in East Anglia,* Professor Whitelock examines pre-Conquest and later evidence relating to the Church in East Anglia, emphasising the unreliability of later claims which, she says, "have too often been repeated without indication of their sources as if they were established fact."*

The kingdom of East Anglia was the largest in south east England, comprising the present day counties of Norfolk, Suffolk, the Isle of Ely and parts of Cambridgeshire east of the Devil's Dyke. Jewellery and other archaeological finds reveal a similarity between Kentish and East Anglian culture. It was the discovery in

---

*Anglo-Saxon England. 1972. Frank Stenton.

1939 of the royal ship burial at Sutton Hoo in Suffolk, with its wealth of exquisite treasure, which has contributed to the theory that, through trade with Kent, Sweden, the Continent and Mediterranean countries, East Anglia had achieved a high degree of material prosperity by the seventh century. But this, of course, was mainly confined to the royal house and higher ranks of society and was not widespread throughout the kingdom. There must have existed in East Anglia some exceptionally gifted craftsmen, for in addition to a number of items in the hoard which are of foreign origin, the fine pieces of gold jewellery inlaid with garnets, coloured glass and shell, were almost certainly made in a local East Anglian workshop attached, most likely, to the royal court itself. Referring to these gold objects Sir Frank Stenton has said, "At least they prove that Kent was not the only heathen kingdom in which the decorative arts were practised with brilliant success."*

The early settlers in East Anglia were a sea-faring people who had come from Schleswig-Holstein and Frisia. It is not surprising that they chose the coastal regions of East Anglia with its many river estuaries in which to settle. They established their royal seat at Rendlesham in Suffolk between the estuaries of the Alde and the Deben by means of which they had probably entered the country. The estuaries could be used by sea-going craft to bring goods into the kingdom from the neighbouring kingdom of Kent and from the Continent. A royal fleet of ships would also have been moored on the river near Rendlesham, one being reserved perhaps for the use of the missionary bishop. We know that the rivers of eastern England were used extensively in Anglo-Saxon England as a means of travel. It is certain that Bishop Felix was in close contact with the court at Rendlesham for he received strong support in his work from the East Anglian kings.

In the chapters that follow we shall see that close ties existed between the royal house of East Anglia and that of Northumbria with the result that the churches of the two kingdoms were also closely associated. The activities of Bishop Felix of East Anglia and Bishop Aidan of Lindisfarne in Northumbria ran concurrently and Bede's statement that Felix had a high regard for Aidan suggests more than a knowledge of him by hearsay; Felix most likely visited Aidan in his Northumbrian see.

---

*Anglo-Saxon England.

Pagan deities of classical mythology. Mercury found at Manea Fen, Cambridgeshire, Venus Colchester, Essex, and Mars at Barkway, Hertfordshire.

Cambridge Museum of Archaeology and British Museum

Lullingstone Roman villa, wall painting showing Christian symbols.   *British Museum*

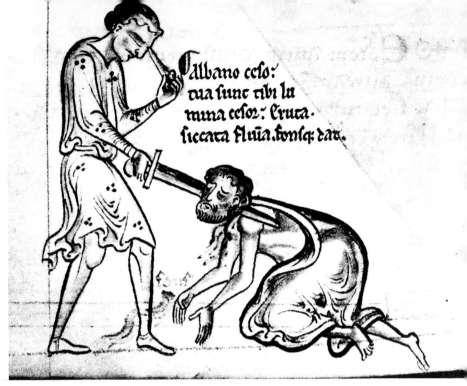

Albano cefo?
tua funt tibi lu
mina cefoz. Cruta.
ficcata fluua.tonfq: dar.

(iii) Martyrdom of St Alban from the thirteenth century *Chronica Maiora*, Matthew Paris. Legend claims that executioner's eyes dropped out as he severed Alban's head so that he should no witness the martyrdom: he is seen here catching his eyeballs.

Corpus Christi College, Cambridge

(iv) Roman theatre at Verulamium (now St Albans).

Chris Age

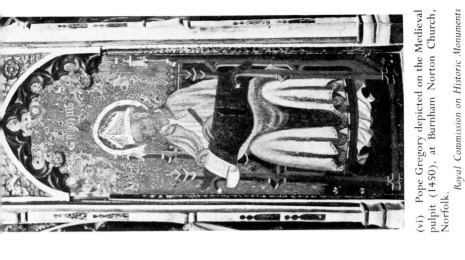

(vi) Pope Gregory depicted on the Medieval pulpit (1450), at Burnham Norton Church, Norfolk.

Royal Commission on Historic Monuments

(v) Fourth Century Roman mosaic from Hinton-St-Mary, Dorset.

British Museum

(vii)   St Augustine's Abbey, Canterbury. On right is north wall of Norman nave and remains
of the Ethelbert tower.   *Richard Cuthbert*

(viii)   Miniatures from the Gospels of St Augustine. Sixth century. Scenes from the Life of Christ
Top row: Entry into Jerusalem; Last Supper; Prayer in Gethsemane. Bottom row: Raising of
Lazarus; Feet washing; The Betrayal.   *Corpus Christi College, Cambridge*

(x) Example of the clear uncial script in which the Gospels of St Augustine are written. This shows St Mark XII v 10 onwards.

Corpus Christi College, Cambridge

(ix) St Augustine's Cross erected in 1884 at Ebbsfleet, Kent, to mark the traditional landing site of Augustine in Britain.

Richard Cuthbert

(xi)   Canterbury Cathedral today.

Richard Cuthber

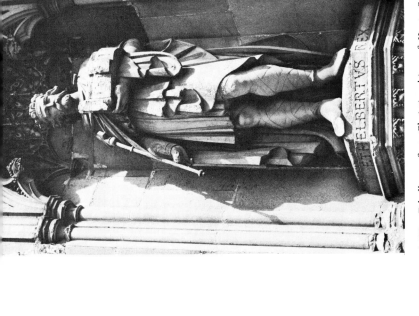

(xiii) Ethelbert, first Christian king of Kent. South front Canterbury Cathedral. *Richard Cuthbert*

(xii) Pope Gregory, West Newton Church, Norfolk. *Margaret Gallyon*

(xv) Parish Church of St Mary and St Eanswyth, Folkestone.

Halksworth Wheeler Studios, Folkestone

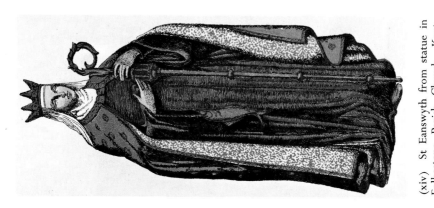

(xiv) St Eanswyth from statue in Folkestone Parish Church, Kent, painted by Miss Roberts

By kind permission of the Vicar, Rev. P. Cole

The first signs that East Anglia was likely to repudiate idolatry and become a Christian kingdom occurred in the first quarter of the seventh century when Redwald was king. He received baptism in Kent, due to the persuasions of King Ethelbert, his overlord. But the baptism was a perfunctory and meaningless rite to Redwald and on his return to East Anglia he continued to worship pagan gods. Christ was to him but one extra god who must be paid respect in case he had power to bring him good fortune and military success. Even while Ethelbert of Kent was Bretwalda, Redwald was rising to power and when Ethelbert died in 616 Redwald succeeded to that position. The Sutton Hoo ship burial could be associated with Redwald and if so, its treasure might well reflect the splendour of his court. Bede describes him as a man of noble birth but ignoble in his deeds. His shallow interest in the new religion is demonstrated by his readiness to yield to his wife's influence for she encouraged him to continue worshipping Thunor and Woden. But he preserved a semblance of Christian belief by placing a Christian altar in the same temple as one dedicated to pagan deities. While he ruled in East Anglia the kingdom remained in heathen darkness and no missionaries were invited to teach his people. If his wife's influence in religious affairs had been as salutary as it was in state affairs the Church might at that time have made some headway in the kingdom. By her good advice she saved her husband from a most treacherous act against another royal personage. Edwin, heir to the throne of Deira (Yorkshire) had been driven from his province by the powerful King Ethelfrid of Bernicia (Northumberland), a neighbouring province. Edwin was given protection and friendship by East Anglia's King Redwald, but when Ethelfrid discovered the hiding place of the fugitive he offered Redwald large bribes in exchange for either the murder or the surrender of Edwin. Redwald, tempted by the bribes, would have complied with Ethelfrid's demands had he not been persuaded by his wife to abandon such a wicked deed. She told him that it was most unworthy and dishonourable for so great a king as her husband to sell his best friend for gold. Moved by his wife's words, Redwald not only refused to surrender the young prince but raised an army, killed Ethelfrid on the battlefield and restored Edwin to the throne of the entire Northumbrian kingdom. Edwin's contact with the East Anglian court continued after Redwald's death for it was through his influence and persuasion that Redwald's son and successor, Eorpwald, repudiated his pagan beliefs and embraced the new religion which was now spreading rapidly to every kingdom in Britain. But soon after his conversion and before the Faith had made any impact on East Anglia Eorpwald was murdered by a pagan usurper, Ricbert, and for three years the kingdom remained heathen.

The significant name in connection with the final conversion of East Anglia is King Sigbert, brother, or more likely half brother, of Eorpwald, for it was during Sigbert's reign, beginning in about AD 630, that missionaries came from the Continent and from Ireland to preach the Faith of Christ in East Anglia. Students of English place names tell us that in East Anglia there is an almost complete absence of names which have a pagan origin. This fact has led to the suggestion that the population responded so favourably and completely to the new teaching that everything associated with paganism was obliterated from the kingdom and that there were no subsequent reversions to the old pagan faith. But in this connection Sir Frank Stenton has said, "it must be left an open question whether their rarity in this country is due to the lethargy of popular heathenism, to changes in nomenclature brought about by later Danish settlement or to the deliberate obliteration of heathen memorials by unusually zealous Christian kings."*

King Sigbert is described by Bede as "a devout Christian and a man of learning". He had been converted to the Faith while he was an exile in Gaul. The reason for his exile is not certain; Bede merely states that it was due to Redwald's hostility towards him. Charles Plummer suggests that perhaps he had political claims which Redwald considered dangerous. When the threat to his safety had been removed by the death of Redwald and when Eorpwald had been treacherously murdered, Sigbert returned to England to govern his kingdom of East Anglia. His first concern was to see the Christian Gospel preached to his people and schools established for their education, such as he had seen in Gaul. He looked to Canterbury for aid in the enterprise and the archbishop, now Honorius, sent him a missionary bishop named Felix, who had come to Canterbury from his native home, Burgundy in Gaul or France as it was now called. Here in Burgundy he had received training for the priesthood and probably also episcopal ordination, though this is not certain. The facts given by Bede in connection with Felix are tantalizingly

*Anglo-Saxon England.

meagre, though later historians have attempted to expand the narrative to cover some details of his life in Burgundy.

One suggestion which is of particular interest is that Felix may have been connected with the mission of Columbanus in Burgundy.* This celebrated Irish missionary had left his monastery at Bangor, where he had been principal master in the schools, and with a band of twelve monks had come to Burgundy where he founded monasteries, the most famous being at Luxeuil. His Rule, though extremely rigorous, was widely adopted in the monasteries of western Europe until it was superseded by the gentler Rule of St Benedict. A fiery character, uncompromising in his concern for truth and moral integrity, Columbanus found himself in conflict with both Church and State: with the Church because of his stubborn adherence to Celtic customs and with the State because of his stern denunciation of the immorality of the Burgundian court. Driven from Burgundy by the fury of Queen Brunhild, whose bastard great-grandchild he had refused to bless, Columbanus travelled to north Italy where he founded a monastery at Bobbio which was destined to become one of the most important centres of piety and learning in medieval Europe. He died in 615.†

If Bishop Felix had not been directly connected with Columbanus' missionary movement in Burgundy it is certain that he must have known of this remarkable Irishman who was making such a marked impression on the Church of his day. A further suggestion has been made that King Sigbert's conversion and religious training in France had been due also to Columbanus and that the king may have been attached to his famous monastery at Luxeuil, where he was so impressed by the teaching in the schools that he wished to make them a model for his own school in East Anglia. It is open to conjecture whether the exiled Sigbert had become acquainted with Felix in Burgundy; nor is it certain that he invited Felix to preach the Faith in his kingdom. Bede's narrative implies that Felix came to England quite independently of Sigbert and that he was already a bishop on arrival. When Felix went to Canterbury Archbishop Honorius sent him to East Anglia where, because of Redwald's apostasy and Eorpwald's murder the Faith had so far gained no hold on the kingdom.

---

*Councils and Ecclesiastical Documents. Haddan and Stubbs.

† Sancti Columbani Opera. G. S. Walker.

Bede states that Felix was bishop of East Anglia for seventeen years and reaped a rich harvest of believers, delivering the province from its unhappiness and wickedness, and in accordance with the mystical meaning of his name, he bestowed upon it the gift of eternal felicity. His missionary base and episcopal seat was established at Dommoc which has traditionally been associated with Dunwich on the south Suffolk coast, now a small village but once a large and prosperous town. It may well be that the tradition is trustworthy and that Dunwich, which still has its bishop, was the site of Felix's cathedral and monastery.

This view, however, has recently been challenged by Mr S. E. Rigold, Inspector of Ancient Monuments for the Department of the Environment. He expressed his own views in a paper entitled *The Supposed See of Dunwich.** After examining primary and later documents relating to the see he asserts that Dommoc is more probably to be identified with Walton Castle near Felixstowe than with Dunwich. He refers to a chronicle of a thirteenth century monk of Norwich, Bartholomew Cotton, a native of Cotton, near Stowmarket, in Suffolk, who would have had access to any surviving documents and a knowledge of local traditions relating to the see. Cotton records that Felix was "buried at Dommoc" adding the gloss "which is now called Filchestowe on the sea in the eastern part of Suffolk." The gloss would, if Cotton is right, suggest that Dommoc is to be equated with Felixstowe, a place which perhaps preserves the founder's name, Felix. Mr Rigold believes that Walton Castle, which adjoins Felixstowe, is a much more likely site than Dunwich for the bishop's seat, for in Roman times it was the site of one of the Saxon Shore forts. These forts with their ready made walls and ample supply of building materials were frequently used by Christian missionaries in the seventh century for the establishment of religious settlements. We know for certain that the forts at Reculver, Richborough, Burgh Castle and Bradwell were converted for Christian purposes. Walton Castle was closer, and therefore more accessible than Dunwich, to the royal capital of Rendlesham and as we have seen, the conversion of East Anglia was achieved by the joint efforts of both king and bishop. Dommoc then, says Mr Rigold, may possibly preserve the lost Roman name of Walton Castle, but, he concludes "the final test of excavation can no longer be applied for both Walton

---

*Journal of British Archaeological Association. 1961. But see also *The Pre-Viking Age Church in East Anglia*. D. Whitelock in *The Anglo-Saxons*. 1972.

Castle and Dunwich have been swallowed by the sea." In the light of this recent research the Ordnance Survey Map, *Britain in the Dark Ages,* printed in 1966, sites Dommoc, the bishop's seat, at Felixstowe, with no reference to Dunwich.

In addition to the establishment of a missionary base on the eastern side of the province, either at Dunwich or Felixstowe, there is a tradition that a second religious foundation of Felix existed on the western side of the province, at Soham, in the Isle of Ely. The sheer size of the diocese and the consequent problem of spreading the Faith to all areas makes this appear very probable. The source of this tradition, older than the Dunwich one, is a twelfth century Chronicle of Ely known as *Liber Eliensis* of which the two most important manuscripts are at Trinity College, Cambridge and Ely Cathedral. There is some uncertainty as to the authorship of the work which has traditionally been attributed to a monk of Ely named Thomas, but a more likely author is the learned monk Richard who became prior of the monastery in 1177.* Much of the early material is based on Bede with a few pieces of local tradition incorporated into it, for instance the founding of a monastery at Seham by Bishop Felix, a place which has usually been identified with Soham in Cambridgeshire. The *Ely Chronicle* records that Felix's body was buried at Soham, presumably after translation from Dommoc, its original place of burial. Later it was again translated to Ramsey Abbey. Excavations at Soham have revealed vestiges of ancient buildings opposite to the present church; though these are not likely to date from the seventh century it is probable that Felix built a church and monastery on the site. In the present church is a fourteenth century wall painting of a mitred figure with hand raised in blessing, thought to represent St Felix.

The cult of the saints was strong in the Middle Ages and wherever a town or village could in some way claim connection with a saint, however flimsy the evidence for such a connection, it did so. Babingly in Norfolk cherishes a tradition that Felix landed there and founded the first church in East Anglia on the site of the existing ruined church of St Felix which stands among the "Christian Hills." Shernborne church nearby also claims to have connections with East Anglia's saint. Counter claims are made by the folk of Felixstowe who assert that theirs

---

Liber Eliensis. Edited by E. O. Blake.

was the landing site of the saint. Walton, the adjoining parish, originally dedicated its church to Felix and we have seen that Walton may have been the original site of his episcopal seat. Even as far north as the North Riding of Yorkshire, the village of Felixkirk claims to have connections with Bishop Felix. As we have mentioned already, Felix most likely travelled northwards and met Bishop Aidan in his Northumbrian see. It would be a mistake to dismiss these and other claims of connections with the saints as mere inventions of pious people who wished to enhance the reputation of their church or village; the claims may very occasionally have a genuine foundation. Although the missionary saints usually exercised their ministry from a permanent base, they also conducted preaching missions, touring the countryside and visiting a variety of places. This is particularly true of the itinerant preachers of the Celtic Church who, like Aidan and Chad, covered many miles on foot, preaching and ministering to the heathen and establishing churches up and down the country. We must remember that there were no districts with heavy concentrations of people such as we have in towns today. Anglo-Saxon England was sparsely populated and the people lived in scattered villages and small settlements. It is likely, then, that some of the traditions connecting local saints with particular places are authentic and that they did in fact land, visit, preach, baptize or found churches in the various places where the claims are made.

An early fourteenth century *Chronicle* of Ramsey Abbey gives a graphic account of how Felix's body was conveyed from Soham to Ramsey by the monks of the latter monastery. The journey was made by boat through the winding waterways of the fens. When the brethren had stolen the sacred relics from Soham and were on their return journey, the monks of Ely, a few miles from Soham, heard of the theft and instantly set out in their boats to give chase to the thieves, but their attempt to locate them was foiled by a dense fog that enveloped the fens. Thus hidden by the fog the brethren of Ramsey were able to reach their abbey without further trouble from the monks of Ely. The relics were solemnly enshrined at Ramsey Abbey and attracted throngs of pilgrims throughout the Middle Ages. Recent archaeological excavations in the abbey precincts have revealed some interesting medieval tiles bearing depictions of St Felix and St Ivo. These are now in St Ives Museum.

The story of King Sigbert who supported and encouraged Felix is of no less interest than that of the bishop himself. He was evidently a scholar and impressed by the schools he had seen in France. He wished to establish similar schools in East Anglia and was able, with the help of Felix, to procure teachers from Canterbury. When Sigbert was satisfied that the foundations of Christian devotion and learning had been laid in his kingdom he felt able to turn his mind to his own cherished desire to enter a monastery. His kinsman, Egric, already shared the government of East Anglia with him and he was now well able to assume complete responsibility for it. So Sigbert surrendered his political power and royal possessions, received the tonsure and entered a monastery of his own foundation. Bede does not name the monastery; it may have been at Burgh Castle near Yarmouth for he had given this site to the Irish missionary Fursey for the founding of a monastery.* But tradition is in favour of identifying the monastery with that at Bury St Edmunds. In the Ely manuscript of *Liber Eliensis* the name Betrichesworde (Bury St Edmunds) has been inserted in the text, which may point to a local tradition that it was to Bury St Edmunds that Sigbert retired. He did not remain at the monastery for more than a few years for political events in East Anglia took a turn for the worse when the kingdom came under attack from Mercia's formidable army. Their military prowess and experience on the battlefield made their victory certain and when the East Anglian army saw defeat ahead they appealed to Sigbert, who had once been a distinguished military commander, to leave his monastery and to join the East Anglian fighting forces. They believed that his presence on the battlefield would inspire the men with courage and confidence. But Sigbert had forsaken worldly affairs and so refused to involve himself in war and bloodshed. Those who had been sent to plead with him, paid no heed to his refusal and forcibly dragged him from his monastery and, despite his protests, compelled him to join in the conflict. But Sigbert would not be persuaded to carry any weapons and thus unarmed he was soon killed by the Mercian warriors. His kinsman, King Egric, was also killed and his army heavily defeated. King Sigbert ranks as a Christian martyr for he died bravely, endeavouring to remain loyal to his Christian profession.

The throne of East Anglia now passed to Redwald's nephew, Anna, who was king until his death on the battlefield in 654. Like

---

*The World of Bede. P. Hunter-Blair.

Sigbert before him he was a devout Christian and eager to see the Faith flourishing in his kingdom. In these two kings, Sigbert and Anna, we see exhibited the two types of Christian piety, always held in respect by the Church: Sigbert, the celibate and ascetic, with his leaning towards monastic life, and Anna practising his Christian Faith within the framework of his secular occupation, married and the father of a Christian family. Bede describes Anna as "an excellent man of royal stock and father of a distinguished family." and again, "a very devout man, noble in mind and deed." Not only did Anna himself promote Christianity in his realm by supporting the work of Bishop Felix and the Irish missionary Fursey, but his four daughters and a step-daughter were also to have a considerable influence on the religious life of East Anglia, Kent and the Continent. His daughter Etheldreda, about whom we shall read later, was abbess of the double monastery at Ely; a second daughter, Sexburg, wife of King Earconbert of Kent, founded the minster at Sheppey; Ethelberga was abbess of the double monastery at Faremoutier-en-Brie in France where many English girls went to train for the religious life before such opportunities existed in England; Withburga founded a small community of nuns at East Dereham in Norfolk and Anna's step-daughter Saethryd became abbess of Faremoutier-en-Brie.

It is likely that King Anna had his court at Rendlesham or thereabouts but the *Ely Chronicle* states that his daughter Etheldreda was born at Exning on the Cambridgeshire-Suffolk border and only a few miles from Soham where, as we have said, Felix probably established a monastery. It is possible that among the various royal estates in his kingdom, one was located at Exning. Princess Etheldreda could then have spent her childhood at Exning, was most likely baptized by Bishop Felix and later in life was to found the minster on the nearby Isle of Ely.

King Anna, like his royal predecessors Sigbert and Egric was killed by Mercian warriors. He fell in battle in 654, his death being recorded in the *Anglo-Saxon Chronicle*. The *Ely Chronicle* adds that he was buried at Blythburgh in Suffolk near to the battlefield where he perished, his body being venerated for centuries to come. Archaeologists at one time believed that the cenotaph at Sutton Hoo could have been assembled in honour of King Anna but recently numismatists have re-examined the collection of Merovingian coins found among the treasure and have formed the opinion that the burial took place during the first half of the seventh century and that therefore the king commemorated is unlikely to have been Anna. It is, they say, more likely to have been Redwald, the powerful East Anglian king who held the position of Bretwalda. But research continues and the Sutton Hoo ship burial still presents a number of unsolved problems.*

Bishop Felix had received the backing of King Anna with the result that Christianity became firmly established in the kingdom by the time of the bishop's death in 647. He was succeeded by one of his fellow workers, Thomas, the deacon, who was an Englishman and native of the fenland district of the Gyrwas, which covered the Isle of Ely and parts of Huntingdonshire and Lincolnshire. Thomas died after five years as bishop and was succeeded by Bertgils, otherwise named Boniface, a native of Kent. The fourth bishop was Bisi who was present at the Council of Hertford summoned by Archbishop Theodore. We have seen in Chapter 3 that after this council, Theodore divided the East Anglian see; Bisi had become seriously ill and could no longer administer such a large area. Two new bishops were appointed: Aecci to the original see of Dommoc in the south where lived the south-folk or people of Suffolk and Badwin to Elmham in the north where lived the north-folk or people of Norfolk. It is not certain whether the new see under Bishop Badwin had its headquarters at North Elmham in central Norfolk or South Elmham in north-east Suffolk but North Elmham is the more probable site. Certainly North Elmham was the see by the middle of the tenth century. Recent excavations at North Elmham have confirmed that there was an important settlement there from the beginning of the eighth century, but no traces have been found of the original cathedral church. Like the majority of ecclesiastical and secular buildings of the early and middle Saxon period it was probably built of timber and daub which would soon have disintegrated with the passage of time. It is quite possible that it was built on the same site as the eleventh century cathedral, of which extensive ruins can be seen today.†

---

*The Sutton Hoo Burial Ship. R. Bruce-Mitford.

†For a discussion of North and South Elmham, see Medieval Archaeology. VI-VIII. page 67-108.

5   St Fursey, Pilgrim for Christ

THE conversion of East Anglia was not achieved solely by the labours of Bishop Felix. An Irish missionary named Fursey also settled in the kingdom and preached the Faith to the heathen English. We see in the work of these two men the Continental and Celtic strains of Christianity subsisting side by side in apparent harmony, the missionaries working towards a common goal and both under royal patronage.

If Bishop Felix was an organizer and man of action, labouring steadily in one place for seventeen years, Fursey was cast in a different mould; a visionary and mystic, he had turned his back on his Irish homeland and joined the great company of wayfaring monks, dedicated to a life of pilgrimage and exile for love of Christ.

We have seen how the eminent missionary monk, Columbanus, at the end of the sixth century, forsook the secure life of the monastery at Bangor in Ireland and with twelve companions travelled to Burgundy and other countries of Europe, founding monasteries and proclaiming the Gospel of Christ. He was typical of countless Irishmen who from the sixth to the ninth century left their native land to become wanderers and exiles "peregrini, pro amore Christi." The practice was distinctive of early Irish spirituality, a form of discipline and self-denial, practised for a variety of religious reasons: to find peace for prayer, to follow in the footsteps of the saints and martyrs, to offer devotions at a famous shrine, to atone for sins or, like Columbanus, to preach the Faith to the heathen.

The wayfarer cherished no hope of ever returning to his native land, and the place of his wandering was dictated, not by his own choice, but by divine providence. Like Abraham, the archetype of all wayfarers, who for the love of God left home and kindred and journeyed into a strange land, the Christian 'peregrinus' turned his back on his homeland and followed where his destiny led him. A striking example of this total abandonment to providence is recorded in the *Anglo-Saxon Chronicle*. In the year 891 "three Irishmen came to King Alfred in a boat without oars, from Ireland, whence they had stolen away, because they wished for the love of God to be on pilgrimage, they cared not where. The boat in which they set out was made of two and a half hides, and they had taken with them provisions for a week and after a week they came to land in Cornwall."*

Such a pilgrim was Fursey, who came to eastern England afire with zeal to preach the Faith to our pagan forefathers. Descended from the royal house of Munster, as a boy, he applied his mind assiduously to his studies and disciplined himself to observe the precepts of the Christian Faith. His early aptitude for prayer and ascetic discipline led him, as a young man, to build a monastic cell for himself on the shores of Lough Corrib in western Ireland where he could devote himself to prayer, fasting and study of the Scriptures. Monasticism at this time flourished in Ireland and, like Fursey, many aspirants to the cloister built their own monastic cells in secluded places, often near to rivers, lakes or the sea. Sometimes these solitary anchorites were joined by other devout souls seeking peace and time for prayer. This necessitated the building of more cells and from such small beginnings the great monastic establishments emerged. Incorporated in the complex of buildings were cells for the monks, a refectory, kitchen, guest room, infirmary, scriptorium, and in the centre of the group stood the church.†

The Latin *Life of Fursey,* of unknown authorship, upon which Bede bases his account of the saint, tells how in his monastic cell in Ireland Fursey fell sick, and how this sickness was the occasion of a heightened spiritual awareness. For the whole of one night his soul seemed to be freed from his body and he was carried by angels to the realms of heaven and hell where he gazed upon sights which filled him with wonder and dread. He saw four raging fires prepared to consume all impenitent sinners and he saw demons flying through the flames, stirring up hatred against the righteous. He saw redeemed souls and saints of his own nation who conversed with him and taught him much of benefit to his soul; and he saw too the torments of a man he had known on earth who died in his sins.‡

---

*Anglo-Saxon Chronicle

† *Early Christian Ireland*. M. and L. Paor.

‡ A detailed account of the vision is given in Bede. III. 19.

The vision was to have a profound effect upon Fursey and those chosen souls to whom he related it. When he had recovered from his illness he began to preach the Faith among his own Irish people. Crowds thronged to hear him and to receive a blessing from him and sometimes to the truly penitent, but not to the merely curious, he would disclose those mysteries of life and death, heaven and hell which had been vouchsafed to him in his visions. His work in Ireland continued for a number of years, until the crowds and the noise began to oppress him. He longed for the stillness that he had known when he first built his cell on the shores of Lough Corrib.

Perhaps this restlessness was a sign that Fursey's work in Ireland was over. Many of his compatriots had forsaken their homeland and become pilgrims for the love of Christ. They had taken to the roads, the forests, the hills and the sea and come to Britain or to the Continent, to France, Germany, Switzerland and Italy. With them they had brought their love of learning, their deep spirituality, their knowledge of monastic rule and discipline, and their creative and artistic skills so beautifully displayed in their illuminated manuscripts. Above all they had brought their Faith to the heathen multitudes. Fursey was resolved to follow in their footsteps. He too would become a pilgrim and an exile for Christ and preach the Faith to the heathen. So with a small company of monks, including his two brothers Foillan and Ultan and the two priests Gobban and Dicul, Fursey left the land of his birth and became a Christian wayfarer, an exile for Christ.

He came eventually, whether by chance or design we cannot tell, to Britain and to East Anglia. Francoise Henry has suggested that Fursey might have come to East Anglia in response to a request from King Sigbert for an Irish missionary to help with the conversion of his kingdom.* This seems very likely in view of the fact that Sigbert had had some connections with Irish missionaries in Burgundy. Dr Henry points out that the kingdom of Northumbria was following a similar policy by inviting Irish monks to preach the Faith to their people. From the Irish community at Iona came Bishop Aidan to Northumbria in response to an appeal from King Oswald. It is possible that Fursey, while still in Ireland had heard of King Sigbert's request for Irish missionaries, or he had perhaps reached Iona or some other settlement of Irish monks on the west

---

*Dark Age Britain. Edited by D. B. Harden.

coast of Britain and received word of East Anglia's need. Alternatively his wanderings may have brought him by chance to East Anglia some weeks or months after he left Ireland. As we have seen, the element of uncertainty as to their ultimate destination was an essential feature of the Irish peregrinations and Bede says of Fursey, "His purpose was to spend his life as a pilgrim for love of our Lord, and to go wherever he found an opening." But whatever the circumstances of his arrival in East Anglia in about AD 631 or soon after he was welcomed by King Sigbert who was glad to receive further help in the task of converting his heathen subjects to the Faith of Christ.

By the wonderful eloquence of his preaching and by the holiness of his life Fursey soon made a number of converts to the new religion, and those who already believed were confirmed in their faith. During these early days in East Anglia, Fursey was once more privileged to receive divine revelations from which he gained great comfort and encouragement. He was urged, in his vision, to continue steadfastly preaching the Word of God, to persevere in his own religious devotions and not to grow weary in well doing. Death was certain for him, as for all men, but the time of its approach was unpredictable, "Watch therefore, for ye know neither the day nor the hour."

King Sigbert, delighted at Fursey's success, had given him land for the establishment of a permanent settlement in East Anglia and on this site Fursey began to build a monastery for himself and his few companions. The site was a disused fortress which the English people called Cnobheresburg, and which tradition connects with the Saxon Shore fort at Burgh Castle near Yarmouth; in Roman times it guarded the estuaries of the Yare and the Waveney. Excavations there have brought to light, as well as Roman coins and material, Saxon pottery, an early Christian cemetery and remains of ecclesiastical buildings which may have been part of Fursey's original monastery or of the larger one built in later years. The ruined fort is now in the hands of the Department of the Environment and visitors may still see its outer walls and huge bastions. Near to the fort is Burgh Castle's parish church with its Saxon-Norman round tower and incorporated into the fabric fragments of Roman tiles and bricks from the fort. In the south wall of the church's nave is a stained glass window of nineteenth century date portraying St Fursey with his distinctive Celtic tonsure.

The site of Fursey's monastery, stark and desolate, was one which must have rejoiced the saint's heart. The sea lay to one side and thick forest to the other. Apart from timber, ample building material was available from the ruined fort, of which a great deal more must have been standing in Fursey's day, thirteen centuries ago. The monastic buildings and the organization and discipline of the monastery would almost certainly have been based on those monasteries he had known in Ireland. Monastic rules of the Celtic branch of the Church were strict and laid emphasis on penance and ascetic discipline. The Rule of Columbanus was especially rigorous: "Let the monks' food be poor and taken in the evening, such as to avoid repletion, and their drink such as to avoid intoxication," and again, "Let him come weary to his bed and sleep walking, and let him be forced to rise while his sleep is not finished."* How much more humane was Benedict's Rule which prescribed sufficient sleep for the brethren and an injunction that they should encourage one another when rising.

There were times when Fursey would be moved to relate to those who would benefit from hearing them, the strange and marvellous visions which from time to time he had received. Bede has left us an endearing picture of the saint recounting his visions to a "truthful and devout man" who met Fursey in East Anglia. The time was winter, frosty and bitterly cold. Accustomed to austerity, Fursey was dressed only in a thin worn garment which could have afforded little protection from the severe weather. But when he spoke of his visions the sweat poured from him as if it had been a hot day in midsummer, so moved was he by the recollection of what he had seen and heard. Bede had every confidence in the truth of the story for it was told him by one of the aged monks in his own monastery at Jarrow.

The portrayal of Fursey in the fifteenth century stained glass window, until recently in Blythburgh church in Suffolk, in which the saint is dressed in a rich green garment with a jewelled mitre on his head, his fingers bedecked with rings, presents a contrast to the austere and simple figure described by Bede. But no doubt on ceremonial occasions when Fursey was arrayed in all his episcopal finery he could look as splendid as the figure in the stained glass window. Unfortunately the window is no longer in

---

*Sancti Columbani Opera. G. S. Walker.

the church. It was still there at the end of the nineteenth century for a painting of it was made then by Hamlet Watling and is in a collection of his paintings at the Christchurch Mansion Museum, Ipswich.

Ipswich Museum also possesses one of a large number of bronze hanging bowls which have been unearthed in Britain from time to time. Their use is uncertain but they may have been used for liturgical purposes. The bowl at Ipswich, dating from the sixth or seventh centuries, bears a scroll design with an inlay of millefiori enamel, typical of Celtic art. It is possible that this bowl and those found in the Sutton Hoo treasure are the product of a workshop at Fursey's monastery in Suffolk for, as Dr Henry says, there were very likely skilled craftsmen among Fursey's band of monks.* Alternatively the bowls could have been brought over to England from Ireland. Dr Henry is of the opinion that the bowls are of Irish origin and were either made in Ireland or in areas of Britain where Irish craftsmen had settled. The objection to the theory that the bowls were made exclusively in Ireland rests upon the fact that few have been discovered in Ireland whereas many have been found in England.†

We have referred to the depiction of Fursey in Blythburgh church in which he is seen in what looks like episcopal attire though the caption in the window designates him as abbot. He was certainly abbot of his monasteries in Ireland, East Anglia and France but it is by no means certain that he was also a bishop though in the Celtic Church the two offices were sometimes combined. Neither in Bede nor in the earliest Latin *Life,* which Bede used, and which was written between 670 and 675, not long after Fursey's death, is his ecclesiastical status mentioned.‡ If he was in fact a bishop, as some later accounts of his life state, this need not have been a cause of any conflict with Bishop Felix for both men were working in East Anglia with the full authority and backing of King Sigbert and both shared the common purpose of winning pagan souls to the Faith of Christ. There were also differences between the pattern of organization in the Roman or Continental Church and the Celtic Church. Roman bishops were under the direct authority of the pope and, if in England, under the authority also

---

*Dark Age Britain. Edited by D. B. Harden.

† The Anglo-Saxons. David Wilson.

‡ Venerabilis Baedae, Latin Text and Notes, III. 19. C. Plummer.

of the archbishop of Canterbury. They had jurisdiction over clearly defined territorial sees (Latin. sedes = seat) and their cathedral church and residence were at some central place in the diocese, often near to the king's court, as at Canterbury in Kent. The Celtic Church on the other hand had no archbishops, and bishops were answerable to no central authority for there was none. Neither did they function in clearly defined territorial areas and their place of residence was the monastery, where, like Bishop Chad of Lastingham, they could hold the rank of both abbot and bishop.

We have seen how King Sigbert retired from political life, became a monk either at Burgh Castle or Bury St Edmunds and not long after was killed during a Mercian invasion of East Anglia, his kinsman Egric being slain too. The devout King Anna was the next to reign over East Anglia; he too encouraged the work of Fursey and made improvements to his monastery, bestowing many gifts upon him and his fellow monks. Gradually through the combined efforts of Felix and Fursey the grip of paganism loosened its hold over the people and we hear of no reversions to belief in the old gods, though in places and among the uneducated peasants there must have lingered a superstitious attachment to traditional and pagan customs which were part of the Anglo-Saxon heritage.

Within the framework of Celtic and Roman monasticism there existed an Order of Anchorites; because of its call to solitude, extreme austerity and advanced forms of prayer it was regarded as a higher state than attachment to a community, but those who embraced it usually did so after a period of training and preparation within the community.* Such an anchorite was Fursey's brother, Ultan, who had come with him from Ireland. He had for many years been attached to a community but then aspired to live the life of an anchorite or hermit. He found a place of quiet and solitude, perhaps, like Guthlac of Crowland, in the remote marshes of the fen country. Here he devoted himself to prayer and fasting and manual labour. Fursey too had a leaning towards this kind of life and after ruling the monastery at Burgh Castle for about ten years and preaching the Faith up and down the country he decided to join his brother at his lonely retreat. His other brother Foillan, a bishop, was well able to manage the affairs of

---

*The Age of Saints in the Early Celtic Church. N. Chadwick. See also the Rule of St Benedict. Translated J. McCann.

the monastery, and Fursey made him abbot. The two priests Gobban and Dicul also shared in the responsibility of the monastery and the care of souls in the district. Having settled the affairs of the community at Burgh Castle Fursey went in search of his brother Ultan. Bede tells us that for a year Fursey "shared his life of prayer and austerity, supporting himself by daily manual labour."

But East Anglia was a troubled and uneasy kingdom and peace was never certain for long. At any time it was likely to suffer attack from the neighbouring kingdom of Mercia. Fursey himself had seen the death of two of East Anglia's kings, Sigbert and Egric, at the hands of the ruthless Mercian warriors. Penda still ruled the kingdom; a pagan himself, he cared little for the Christian missionaries or the conversion of his kingdom, though he did not forbid the preaching of the Faith to his people; but it made little headway in Mercia until his death in 655. Fursey could forsee that if Penda's army overran the kingdom of East Anglia no mercy would be shown to the Christians. What would become of their monasteries and churches, their books and their treasures? He shrank from the thought of such devastation. Perhaps there was more future for him and his brothers in France; many of his fellow Irishmen had gone there to preach the Gospel or to found monasteries; only fifty or so years before, Columbanus had been at work there, and every Irish monk sought to emulate this saintly missionary. Had not Fursey dedicated himself to a life of pilgrimage and exile? Perhaps there lurked in his restless soul a yearning for that heavenly country which had figured so vividly in his visions leaving its indelible imprint on his sensitive mind. For Fursey, that country did not lie far ahead, but first there was work for him to do in France, where he was to win even greater fame, though largely posthumous, than in either Ireland or Britain. Bishop Felix who had himself worked in Burgundy most likely had a share in influencing Fursey's decision to travel to France.

In about 644, the precise date is not known, Fursey settled his affairs in Britain and crossed over to France. He arrived in Neustria, the north west region, with Paris as its chief city. He was hospitably received by the king, Clovis II and his wife Bathild, an English woman of rare beauty who had come to France as a slave and had been purchased from the slave market by the king's chief minister, Earconwald. As manager of the king's estates Earconwald gave Fursey some land at Lagney on the river Marne and here Fursey built a monastery and ministered to the needs of the community in the district as well as ruling the monastery as abbot. After it was well established Fursey felt able to leave for a while to visit his brothers in East Anglia for he had left them there at a time of strife and uncertainty. He set out on his journey from Lagney but reached no further north than Mezerolles when he was struck down by sickness. He was nursed in a monastery of Irish monks but died soon after, either in 649 or 650.

But death did not bring an end to Fursey's fame for his friend and benefactor, Earconwald, happened at that time to be building a church on his own private estate at Péronne in Picardy and he secured the saint's body and buried it in a side chapel which had already been completed; this he thought would ensure that Fursey's name would be remembered and honoured and the Abbey of Péronne would win renown. According to legend a dispute arose between Earconwald and two other claimants of the body, but providence intervened to show clearly that it was destined to rest at Péronne for the bullocks pulling the cart which bore the coffin refused to go in any other direction but Péronne.* Fursey's body, then, was interred in the church at Péronne and a month later removed to a place near the high altar. After four years it was exhumed again in order to be placed in a shrine where pilgrims could come to honour the saint. The exhumation revealed the body to be free from corruption, a true sign, it was believed, of Fursey's sanctity, further proof of which was afforded by the many miracles which occurred at his shrine.

Pilgrims, especially from Ireland, began to flock to Péronne and the abbey gained a high reputation for its piety and learning. A correspondence has survived from the late seventh century between Cellanus, the Irish abbot of Péronne and Aldhelm, the English scholar and abbot of Malmesbury in Wiltshire. The literary style of Cellanus's letter is elaborate and verbose and reflects the influence of Aldhelm's equally ornate style, for Cellanus was an avid reader of Aldhelm's works. He writes, "I, an Irishman, living unknown in the further corner of Frankish land, exile from a renowned community, the lowest and most unworthy servant of Christ, in the one and wondrous Trinity, I bid you greeting. . . If you would comfort the sadness of a stranger in a foreign land, send me a few sermons in your own beautiful style, that the streams drawn from this clear spring may gladden the minds of many, in

---

*The Wandering Saints. Eleanor Duckett.

this place where Saint Fursey rests his sacred body, untouched by decay."*

Many memorials of Fursey survive in France today both at Lagney where he founded his monastery and at Péronne where his body was buried. These memorials, including the holy well connected with the saint, his alleged skull, the chapel of Fursey at Lagney, and so on, are described by Margaret Stokes in her book *Three Months in the Forests of France* which she wrote in 1895 after a pilgrimage to the various sites connected with the early Irish saints.

But much of Fursey's fame has arisen from that unusual feature of his deeply religious nature which made him receptive to divine revelations. From the manuscripts dealing with his life, the visions were singled out as being of special interest and importance and separate copies of them were made, distributed and widely studied. Like the visions of the monk of Melrose, St Drycthelm, which are also related by Bede, Fursey's visions were among the earliest examples of a type of literature which became both popular and profuse in the Middle Ages, reaching its climax in the superb fourteenth century work of Dante, the *Divine Comedy,* influenced almost certainly by these earlier works. This type of literature dealt with the future life and the fate of departed souls, its imagery drawn from classical and oriental mythology or from Jewish and Christian apocalyptic writings.† One of the finest and earliest examples of this type of literature, which was to have a great influence on future work, was the *Vision of Adamnan,* of unknown authorship, probably composed in the tenth century but based on an earlier original work and claiming to be the authentic vision of the seventh century abbot of Iona, Adamnan.

The imagery used in the vision literature is vivid, even crude, but we should remember that, like all imagery, it points to something beyond itself, in this case to the torment of separation from God which is hell, and the bliss of union with Him which is heaven. To Fursey's visions of heaven and hell, and indeed to the whole range of vision literature, we might apply the words of Dorothy Sayers on the use of imagery in the *Divine Comedy.* In the introduction to her translation she writes, "Dante did not

---

Anglo-Saxon Saints and Scholars. Eleanor Duckett.

†*An Irish Precursor of Dante.* C. S. Boswell.

really suppose that Hell was a pit extending from a little way below the foundations of Jerusalem to the centre of the earth, or that Purgatory was a mountainous island in the Antipodes. . .nor did he really imagine that Heaven was located among the celestial spheres. . . He did, however, share the belief of all Catholic Christians that every living soul in the world has to make the choice between accepting or rejecting God, and that at the moment of death it will discover what it has chosen."*

This chapter would be incomplete without further mention of Fursey's two brothers Foillan and Ultan who had settled with him in East Anglia. The monastery at Burgh Castle where Foillan was abbot survived for several years after Fursey's departure to France. But around the middle of the seventh century it was attacked and plundered by Mercian invaders, the monks either escaping or being captured and killed. Foillan and Ultan made their way over to France for safety and came to Péronne where a few years before, their brother's body had been enshrined. Their wanderings, for they too were among Christ's pilgrims and exiles, brought them into Belgium where the famous missionary Amand was at work among the heathen. They found a welcome at the Abbey of Nivelles where the learned and devout Gertrude was mother abbess, and soon they were established in a monastery of their own at Fosse, not far from Nivelles. From here they helped Amand to preach the Faith. In 655 Foillan and three of his fellow monks, while engaged on an errand of mercy, were cruelly murdered by a band of robbers. The bodies of the four monks were discovered by the brethren of Fosse Monastery and brought back for burial there. A touching story is told of Ultan, who succeeded his brother as abbot of the monastery. Gertrude, abbess of Nivelles, feeling that her own death was soon to come about, sent one of her monks to Ultan, who was known to possess powers of prophecy, to enquire when exactly her death was to be. Without hesitation Ultan replied, "Tomorrow, the seventeenth of March, Gertrude, maid of the Lord Christ, shall go upon her way. And bid her, my son, that she fear not, nor be anxious in her going, but depart in joy." The messenger, a little surprised and sceptical said, "Did Heaven tell you this?" to which Ultan replied, "Don't stop to ask questions. Go quickly and tell her. Tomorrow you will find out." Sure enough on the day following Gertrude died.†

---

*The Divine Comedy. Translated D. L. Sayers.

†The Wandering Saints. Eleanor Duckett.

6   Two East Anglian Princesses

1. Etheldreda, Abbess of Ely.

IN THE presbytery of Ely cathedral and in front of the High
Altar, a stone slab, set in the floor, marks the place where there
once stood a richly ornamented shrine containing the relics of one
of the most revered and popular female saints of Anglo-Saxon and
medieval England. The inscription on the slab reads, "Here stood
the shrine of Etheldreda, Saint and Queen, who founded this
House AD 673." Overhead in the vaulted roof is a painted boss
depicting the saint wearing a crown to indicate her royal status and
carrying a crozier, the sign of her spiritual authority over the monks
and nuns of her double minster. Incidents from her life are
beautifully portrayed on the stone corbels at the head of the pillars
in the cathedral's famous Octagon. They show her marriage to
Egfrid, prince of Northumbria, her receiving the veil from Bishop
Wilfrid of York, her consecration as abbess of Ely and so on. Some
of the eight incidents portrayed are undoubtedly historical, others
drawn from the realm of legend, for many legends surround this
mysterious Anglo-Saxon saint. A princess of East Anglia and later
queen of Northumbria, Etheldreda renounced the luxuries of the
court for the austerities of the cloister. She was twice married yet
an ancient tradition claims that she preserved "the glory of
perpetual virginity."

> "Chaste is my song, not wanton Helen's rape.
> Leave lewdness to the lewd! Chaste is my song."*

So sang Bede in his hyme of praise to this bride of Christ, to whom
he devotes a chapter of some length in his *History of the English
Church.*

Bede was a most careful and painstaking historian and Etheldreda
was almost his contemporary; we should therefore examine his
account of her life with the respect it deserves, remembering that
he spent almost the whole of his life in Northumbria and knew its
history well. For twelve years Etheldreda had been the wife of

---

*Bede. IV. 20. Colgrave and Mynors.

Egfrid, prince and later king of Northumbria. Bede, moreover, had talks with Bishop Wilfrid, who was chaplain to the royal couple and had first-hand knowledge of Northumbrian court affairs.

A second source of information on the life of Etheldreda is the *Chronicle of Ely, Liber Eliensis,* to which we have referred, but this, in the early part, contains a good deal of legendary material. The chronicler refers also to "a small book containing her life, written in English," which he very likely used when writing about the saint. This book is unfortunately now lost but that such a book existed, perhaps as a locally produced work, is suggested by two existing Lives of Etheldreda: one a twelfth century manuscript in Corpus Christi College Cambridge, the other a fourteenth century manuscript in Trinity College Dublin. The similarity between the two suggests that they were drawing on a common source which may well have been the lost *Life,* written in English.*

From Bede and the *Ely Chronicle* we gather that Etheldreda was a daughter of the devout King Anna of East Anglia. If the *Ely Chronicle* is to be trusted she was born at Exning in west Suffolk, not far from Ely and Soham, but at the time of her birth Anna was but a prince of the East Anglian court. He did not succeed to the throne until after the death of Sigbert and Egric in about 636 or even later, the date being uncertain. Her birth in 630 coincides with the arrival in East Anglia of Bishop Felix who baptized Anna and his family. Etheldreda, then, was growing up during Felix's missionary activities in the kingdom and was about seventeen when he died in 647. In view of the close association that existed between clergy and rulers in early England it is likely that King Anna and his family received instruction in the Faith from Bishop Felix or members of his missionary band.

The introduction of the Christian Faith to the pagan English came through the preaching of men dedicated to the monastic ideal which meant that Christianity tended to become equated with monasticism. In the outburst of religious fervour which followed the Conversion, the monastic ideal became extremely popular among new converts, resulting in the foundation of a large number of monasteries up and down the country. The impulse towards the religious life was particularly strong among

---

*Introduction. *Liber Eliensis.* Edited by E. O. Blake.

78

women of the royal families who were in close contact with the missionary monks. Sometimes, as in the case of Etheldreda, there must have existed a conflict between their desire for the cloister and their parents' wishes to arrange marriages for them which would be in the political interests of the kingdom. Both of Etheldreda's marriages appear to have been against her will. Unlike her sister Sexburg, who before entering the cloister, married King Earconbert of Kent and fulfilled her duties as queen, wife and mother, Etheldreda could not resign herself to a role for which she felt no inclination.

Her first marriage was to Tonbert, a young earldorman of the Gyrwas, a tribe inhabiting the fenland regions of East Anglia. She married him in about 652 and received from him, as dowry, the Isle of Ely which, according to Bede, lay in the province of East Anglia and was large enough to support six hundred families; it was surrounded by water and marshes and derived its name from the large number of eels which were to be found in the marshes, a feature of the fens which is still evident today. The island later in Etheldreda's life was to become the chief scene of her religious activities, for here she was to found a minster and to preside over it as abbess. Accounts of her virginity, sustained throughout her life, indicate that her marriage to Tonbert was not consummated. But in any case the union, such as it was, ended with Tonbert's sudden death which the *Ely Chronicle* assigns to the year 655 but which Bede says occurred shortly after the marriage.

For five years following Tonbert's death Etheldreda lived at Ely devoting herself to prayer and ascetic discipline. Perhaps it was during these years of widowhood that she formed the idea of making Ely a centre of religious devotion and founding a double minster such as her kinswoman Hilda had founded on the cliff top at Whitby. But Etheldreda's dream was not to become a reality until some years later, for the political situation in East Anglia was unstable and it looked as if another marriage, advantageous to the kingdom, was to be forced upon her. Her father King Anna had been killed in battle in 654 during an invasion of East Anglia by the Mercian army and he was succeeded by his brother Ethelhere who appears to have had pagan sympathies. Instead of resisting the Mercian foe he formed an alliance with Penda and assisted his fighting forces in their attacks against Northumbria, a Christian kingdom ruled by Oswy. But both Ethelhere and Penda perished in the battle of the Winwaed in Yorkshire and a second brother of Anna, Ethelwald, came to the throne of East Anglia. Ethelwald was anxious to re-establish friendly relations between his kingdom and Northumbria where King Oswy had gained the position of Bretwalda and held sway over all the kingdoms south of the Humber. Ethelwald's niece, Etheldreda, was still renowned for her beauty and noble qualities of character and when a marriage between her and Oswy's young son, Prince Egfrid, seemed likely, Ethelwald was eager to encourage it. It was a match which Etheldreda can hardly have anticipated with much enthusiasm for Egfrid was but a youth of seventeen or so and she nearing thirty and still cherishing the hope of taking the veil. But King Ethelwald's wishes prevailed and Etheldreda was married to the Northumbrian prince.

This second marriage took place in 659 or 660, in some part of the Northumbrian kingdom, probably at York. She was accompanied northwards by her attendants and the chief steward of her household, Owini, whose memorial cross, dating, it is thought, from the seventh century, stands in the south aisle of Ely Cathedral and bears the inscription, "Grant, O God, to Owin Thy light and rest. Amen." We hear more of Owini in connection with Lastingham monastery in Yorkshire where he entered as a monk and demonstrated to his fellow monks the dignity of manual labour.

Of the private agreement between Etheldreda and her husband concerning their marital relationship we of course know nothing, but Bede states that she lived with Egfrid for twelve years, while all the time preserving her virginity. People in Bede's day doubted the truth of this rumour and Bede made his own enquiries from Bishop Wilfrid who affirmed that it was indeed true and that Egfrid had appealed to him many times to speak with the queen on the matter and to urge her to consummate the marriage. She would listen, he said, to Wilfrid, for there was no one whom she admired and respected more than him. Wilfrid told Bede that Egfrid had offered him large sums of money and estates if he would agree to speak with the queen and to use his influence to persuade her to honour their marriage bond. What steps Wilfrid took to comply with Egfrid's wishes we do not know, but if we are to believe the *Ely Chronicle* he acted, not on the king's behalf, but on Etheldreda's, encouraging her in her ambition to take the veil. The evidence from various accounts of her life suggests that a strong bond of mutual admiration and understanding existed between Queen Etheldreda and Bishop Wilfrid and that she, a strong and determined character, was much influenced by this distinguished and high-minded churchman. We see her, as queen, making a grant of land to him for a monastery at Hexham, she received the veil from him, she was consecrated abbess of Ely by him and we see him present at the translation of her body to the monastic church. It is likely that if we knew more about her personality, the motives and sentiments which governed her behaviour, the circumstances and political intrigue surrounding her two marriages and the pressures and influences to which she was subjected, we might form a more favourable impression of this saint who on the surface appears as an obstinate and misguided woman with a lack of charity towards her two forbearing husbands. Yet there must have been good reason for her to be widely acclaimed as a saint and she had, no doubt, outstanding qualities of character and had attained to a high degree of virtue. She was single-minded in her dedication to the celibate life, excelling in the virtue of self-discipline and practising the customary austerities which were accepted as the hall-mark of true sainthood; she displayed great patience and meekness during her last illness and after her death, miracles occurred at her tomb which again was considered a sign of genuine sanctity.

Wilfrid's failure to act on behalf of Egfrid and Etheldreda's own persistent requests for release from her marriage ties led eventually to an annulment of her marriage to Egfrid. She was at last free to follow what she believed to be her true vocation and, still remaining in the kingdom of Northumbria, she entered the double monastery at Coldingham on the Berwickshire coast, to train for the religious life and to live according to monastic rule. The monastery at that time was ruled by Ebba, a woman of royal blood and aunt of King Egfrid. It was built on the top of a precipitous promontory now known as St Abb's Head, a place of stark grandeur and devoid of worldly distractions. Here, in the year 672 Etheldreda took the veil.

Her training at Coldingham lasted for a year and in 673 she returned to her native East Anglia and to the Isle of Ely. A number of delightful legends are attached to her return to East Anglia. King Egfrid is said to have regretted freeing her from her marriage ties and with a group of thanes went in pursuit of her just as she was about to leave Coldingham, but an exceptionally high tide foiled his attempt to reach her and she was able to continue her journey southwards without further interference. When she and her maidens had safely crossed the Humber they lay down to rest and Etheldreda thrust her staff into the ground beside her. Later, after waking from sleep, she found that the staff had miraculously burst into foliage, a sign of that spiritual fruition which was to result from her life and work. Both legends are depicted in the stone carvings in the cathedral.

Egfrid had succeeded to the Northumbrian throne in 670 or 671 and married for the second time. Eddius in his *Life of Wilfrid* attributes much of his animosity towards Wilfrid to the influence of his second wife, Eormenberg, who exhibited none of the gentle ways of Etheldreda. She was envious of Wilfrid's great wealth and power and stirred up hatred against him in the king's heart.* Together she and the king contrived to have Wilfrid expelled from his northern bishopric and deprived of his estates and property. Eddius describes how fortune smiled upon the king when he was on friendly terms with Bishop Wilfrid but when he quarrelled with him, trouble ensued. The latter years of his reign were beset by warfare and bloodshed, his young brother Elfwin being killed in the battle of the Trent while Egfrid was waging war against Mercia. Several years later Egfrid sent an invading army into Ireland and launched brutal attacks upon the native inhabitants who had done nothing to deserve such aggression and in the following year 685 he made similar attacks against the Picts though he had been warned by his friends and counsellors against such an action. It was during a battle against the Picts that Egfrid himself was killed, the enemy having feigned defeat and lured him to his death on a narrow mountain pass. Eddius tells us that after his death, his queen, Eormenberg, changed from a she-wolf into a lamb and became abbess of a monastery.

When Etheldreda returned to East Anglia the kingdom was ruled by her cousin Aldwulf, the son of an unknown Ethelric.† His mother was Hereswith, sister of the learned and celebrated Abbess Hilda of Whitby whose double monastery Etheldreda most likely visited while she was in Northumbria and which must to a large extent have provided a pattern for her own monastery at Ely. Hilda's connection with the East Anglian court, through her

*Lives of the Saints. Penguin Classics.

† The East Anglian Kings of the Seventh Century, F. Stenton in The Anglo-Saxons. Edited by P. Clemoes.

sister's marriage to Ethelric, brought her into contact with that kingdom and Bede relates that in 647 when she was about thirty years old, she spent a year in East Anglia intending to join her sister later at the double monastery at Chelles in France. Etheldreda was at that time seventeen years old and her father Anna still ruler of the kingdom. Hilda, a mature and gifted woman no doubt made a strong impression upon the young Princess Etheldreda, who, had she lived long enough, might have achieved a notoriety comparable to that which Hilda herself was later to achieve as abbess of Whitby. Like Hilda, Etheldreda possessed organizing ability as well as personal sanctity and for seven years she governed her great fenland minster as "the virgin mother of many virgins vowed to God." That the minster provided for the training of monks as well as nuns is clear from Bede's account of the translation of Etheldreda's body, when some of the brethren were sent to look for material for making a coffin; and during the ceremony of the translation the whole community was present "the brothers on one side, and the sisters on the other."

We know nothing of the original buildings on their elevated site at Ely. The Ely chronicler relates that Etheldreda restored a church which had been founded there by King Ethelbert of Kent. The monastic buildings were most likely constructed of timber and daub but some of them, the church in particular, of stone. If Wilfrid had been Etheldreda's adviser on the buildings of the monastery they would have been no mean structures for he was noted for his architectural achievements in the north, at York, Ripon and Hexham where, Eddius tells us, the church with its high walls and columns, its numerous side-aisles, its passages and spiral staircases and its crypts of dressed stone, was without parallel on this side of the Alps.

In the double monastery at Ely Etheldreda, as the first abbess, governed her community with wisdom and devotion, guiding and encouraging the brethren and sisters by her sound teaching and virtuous life. Bede relates some of her personal austerities which were commonly practised by many other saints of her day. Vanity in dress was avoided by those dedicated to the religion of Christ. Had not Christ said, "life is more than food, the body more than clothes"? Etheldreda refused to dress herself in expensive materials like linen and would wear only coarse woollen garments. This was a common feature of asceticism. It was said of Bridget, one of Ireland's most popular saints, that "next her skin she wore ever rough and sharp woollen cloth."* And at Lindisfarne in Cuthbert's time the monks were expected to be content to wear natural wool and not to wish for garments of costly material.

Abstinence from the bath was another austerity practised by the saints, though to us it would seem like a failure to pay attention to personal hygiene; but to them, bathing in hot water savoured of luxury and self-indulgence. Etheldreda would take a hot bath only before the major festivals of the Church, such as Easter, Whitsun and Epiphany. These were favourite occasions also for the administration of baptism which suggests that her ablutions at these festival times were not only for the purpose of cleanliness but were commemorative of the washing away of sin in the rite of baptism. Bede tells us that she would assist the other nuns to wash first, which again suggests that this was partly an act of religious devotion, a memorial and imitation of Christ's humble act of washing his disciples' feet. A more precise example of this is found in Bede's *Life of Cuthbert* when the saint welcomed the brethren who visited him on Farne Island and washed their feet in warm water, they in turn doing the same for him; but as a rule Cuthbert kept his boots on from one Easter to the next.

Restraint in eating was another of Etheldreda's austerities; she rarely took more than one meal a day except at the major festivals when a relaxation of the rigours of fasting was permitted. The Rule of St Benedict, which could be adapted for the use of nuns as well as monks, allowed for two meals a day, one main meal and another lighter one. The Rule was introduced by Wilfrid into the northern monasteries and it is likely that he encouraged its use at Ely and advised Etheldreda on its adaptation to the particular needs of her double minster. But at this stage of monasticism in England abbots and abbesses did not govern their monasteries according to a single standard rule, such as that of St Benedict; instead they compiled their own composite rule, derived from a variety of existing rules and adapted to suit the particular needs of their own community. It was not until the monastic revival of the tenth century that uniformity of obedience to the Benedictine Rule was achieved.

Etheldreda, like all the saints, devoted many hours to prayer; she always remained behind in the church after matins until the first light of dawn, matins being said between midnight and 3 a.m.

---

* Venerabilis Bedae. Edited by Mayor and Lumby.

She was endowed too with the spiritual gift of prophecy and fore-told the time and circumstances of her own death and that of others in the monastery. This gift of foreknowledge is accredited to many of the saints and is described in accounts of their lives.

In 680, after ruling the monastery for only seven years, Etheldreda was struck down by a fatal illness which Bede describes as the plague, though some have maintained that it was more likely tuberculosis which caused her death.* Bede records a number of outbreaks of plague in seventh century England. Monasteries were particularly vulnerable because of the large quantities of grain they stored which attracted rats carrying the disease. Infection could also be spread by the monks themselves for they travelled much from one monastery to another. Etheldreda's physician, Cynifrid, described how a large tumour developed under her jaw and that he lanced it to release the poisonous matter from it. She, in a true spirit of humility, said she deserved such an affliction, to atone for her past vanity, for as a girl she had adorned her neck with unnecessary gold and pearls. The operation performed by Cynifrid brought her some relief and for the next two days her condition improved, but then the pain and fever returned and on the third day she died. In accordance with her wishes she was buried in a simple wooden coffin in the monastery graveyard where the other nuns were buried.

After her death the brethren and sisters of the monastery elected her sister Sexburg to succeed her as abbess. She was at the time living as a simple nun at Ely but had founded and ruled the minster at Sheppey and had, therefore, knowledge and experience of monastic administration. The most memorable event of her abbacy was the translation of Etheldreda's body from the grave-yard to the minster church which took place in about 696, sixteen years after she died. Sexburg sent some of the brothers to look for some suitable blocks of stone for making a new coffin. Ely at that time was surrounded by water and marshland and approachable only by boat, hardly the sort of terrain in which the brothers would find stone. But fifteen or so miles south of Ely was a small ruined fortress city built by the Romans. The city was called Grantacaestir, "the Roman fort on the Granta" now known as Cambridge.† The brethren from Ely, therefore, set out in their

---

*The Medical Background of Anglo-Saxon England. W. Bonser.

† Bede. IV. 19. Colgrave and Mynors.

boat and rowed to Cambridge. The Roman settlement was in the Castle Hill area and it is here, most likely, that they found near the city wall and among the fallen masonry of the ancient buildings, a complete marble sarcophagus of beautiful Roman craftsmanship. Elated by this unexpected find the monks took the coffin and its perfectly fitting lid to their boat and made for home. Later it was found that the coffin was exactly the size of the saint's body as if it had been made for her.

Among those present at the translation of Etheldreda's body were Bishop Wilfrid, Cynifrid her physician, the brethren and sisters of the community and many others who had known her. It was the custom on such an occasion to erect a tent over the grave for the actual removal of the body from the ground. Sexburg and a few others went inside, while outside stood the congregation of worshippers singing, the brethren on one side, the sisters on the other. Suddenly from inside the tent the abbess was heard to exclaim "Glory be to the name of the Lord". She summoned Cynifrid to enter and he described later what he saw: there lay Etheldreda as if asleep, her body as pure and free from decay as it had been on the day of her burial sixteen years before, the linen clothes in which she had been wrapped also appearing fresh and clean. But most wonderful to relate, when they lifted the cloth from her face Cynifrid saw that the incision he had made in her neck had entirely healed and instead of the gaping wound which had so disfigured her at the time of her death, there remained only the very faintest scar. Let the reader interpret this as he will. No doubt one could find natural explanations for these phenomena: the loss of body fluids had caused the wound to shrink and close together and the incorruption of the body was due to the use of embalming spices and other substances or to the preservative nature of the peaty soil in which it was buried. But to the people of Bede's day the body's incorruption was a sign of the saint's purity and the healing of the wound a prefiguration of that renewal and restoration which awaits those that are in Christ, "Behold I make all things new."

Etheldreda's body, after being washed and reclothed by the sisters of the community, was reverently laid in the marble coffin and placed near the altar in the minster church. Here at the beginning of the eighth century in Bede's own day it was held in great veneration and like Fursey's shrine at Péronne it attracted throngs of pilgrims, giving to this remote island in the fens an importance it had never known before and making it one of East Anglia's most vital centres of religious devotion.

The monastery, under a succession of abbesses, flourished until 870 when, like other monasteries in eastern England, it was robbed and destroyed by Danish invaders. But a hundred years later it was revived by Aethelwold, bishop of Winchester, Brythnoth being appointed as the abbot. The marble coffin containing the sacred relics, which had survived the destruction, was once more brought into the church and enclosed in a richly ornamented shrine. The *Ely Chronicle* relates how at the beginning of the eleventh century King Canute and his wife Emma frequently visited the abbey at Ely and that the queen gave to the church a purple cloth worked with gold and set with jewels for the shrine of Etheldreda. On one occasion when they were visiting the abbey for the Feast of the Purification the king stood in the royal barge as it neared the abbey church and to his great delight he heard, drifting across the marshes, the sound of the monks chanting their Office. This so pleased him that he too broke into song and urged his thanes to join him.

Etheldreda's popularity in the Middle Ages is indicated by the numerous depictions of her which are still to be seen in our ancient churches, in stained glass, sculptures, and painted screens, and there must have been a great many more of these before the destruction of religious images and paintings by the Puritan iconoclasts of the seventeenth century. Particular prominence was given in church art to local saints and it is not surprising to find Etheldreda frequently portrayed in East Anglian churches. She appears, for instance, on screens at Barnham Broom, Burlingham St Andrew, North Tuddenham, Ranworth, Gately, East Dereham and in the sculptures of Ely Cathedral and the stained glass in Sandringham church. She is depicted in a more crude, but popular form of art, on pilgrim badges of the fourteenth and fifteenth centuries. These small, leaden, souvenir badges were bought by pilgrims at the various shrines of the saints, and worn on the dress or cap as evidence that their wearers had visited the shrines. It was believed too that the badges, which depicted saints, would bring spiritual benefit or physical healing to the wearer. A saint was often depicted with his or her distinctive emblem or perhaps a particular aspect of the saint's life or martyrdom was depicted. St Alban appears with his head hanging from a tree after decapitation, St Edmund is shown being shot at with arrows, St

Etheldreda holds her budding staff and so on. Well over a thousand of these badges portraying various saints have been found in Britain, the majority in London but many also at other important medieval ports such as Ipswich and King's Lynn. A number are displayed in King's Lynn Museum; these were collected by a local jeweller who encouraged children to look for them in the mud of the Fleets where, many years before, in the heyday of pilgrimage, they had been either lost or wantonly discarded by pilgrims.

Ely today is visited by thousands of tourists who come, not as in medieval times to offer their devotions at the saint's shrine or to buy souvenir badges, though we may be sure that religious motives still prompt many visitors to come to our great cathedrals, but to see the magnificent Norman building which now stands on or near the site of Etheldreda's ancient minster. The cathedral, in 1973, celebrated the thirteen hundredth anniversary of its foundation by this saintly princess of the royal house of East Anglia.

2. St Withburga of Dereham

The parish church of Holkham, a village on the north Norfolk coast, stands impressively on a hillock in the park attached to Holkham Hall. It bears a unique dedication to St Withburga, sister of Etheldreda and youngest daughter of King Anna. Though little is known of Withburga, her historicity is attested by her inclusion in the tract known as the *Resting Places of the English Saints,* which occurs, among other places, in the eleventh century *Hyde Register* and refers to her as the daughter of Anna. Sir Frank Stenton believes that the statement "can safely be accepted as a genuine Old English tradition."* If the *Anglo-Saxon Chronicle* is to be trusted for the date it assigns to the discovery of her uncorrupt body she lived to a very great age for we read that in 798 "the body of Wihtburh was found quite sound and free from corruption at Dereham, fifty five years after she departed this life." This would bring her death to 743. But in an earlier entry in the *Chronicle,* the death of her father, King Anna, is recorded as having taken place in 654, which, even if it occurred in her early infancy, would make her about ninety at the time of her own death. The question of her age is complicated further by mention in some accounts of her life that she spent her childhood on the royal estate of Holkham and that not until the death of her father

---

The East Anglian Kings of the Seventh Century, F. Stenton in *The Anglo-Saxons*. Edited by P. Clemoes.

did she move to Dereham where she founded a small convent of nuns.

The dedication of Holkham church to Withburga suggests that the saint had some connection with the place. In the middle of the nineteenth century, when restoration work was being done to the church, as well as remains of a Norman building being found, there was strong evidence for the existence of an even earlier Saxon one on the same site. We may suppose that the original church was built in honour of Withburga and her connection with Holkham, which at one time was named Withburgstowe.*

But Withburga's real fame lies in her association with the Norfolk town of East Dereham where she founded and presided over a community of nuns. Legend tells how at a time of severe food shortage two does from a herd of wild deer attached themselves to the nunnery and supplied the sisters with milk. Then an overseer of the land, envious of Withburga's sanctity and wonder-working powers, hunted the deer with his dogs and drove them off. The scene is depicted in East Dereham's town sign which straddles the High Street. Medieval church artists painted the saint on the screens of many East Anglian churches testifying to her popularity in the district. Paintings survive in the churches at Dereham, Barnham Broom and North Burlingham, all in Norfolk. She is depicted also in the early twentieth century glass in Fritton church, Suffolk. Her distinctive emblem is a deer and she is shown in the paintings and glass with one or two of these animals around her skirts and she is often seen holding a church, as in the bench end in the chancel of Holkham church. Visitors to Holkham Hall, the home of the Earl of Leicester, will find, appropriately, a large herd of fallow deer grazing in the park.

Many tales are told of the miraculous emergence from the ground of springs of clear water in places connected with various saints. When St Alban for instance approached the place of his martyrdom and prayed for water to assuage his thirst, instantly a spring bubbled up at his feet. St Cuthbert, being without a supply of fresh water on Farne Island, prayed to God in his need and when the brethren dug deep into the hard soil, water surged up from below. Withburga is not connected with the emergence of a spring during her lifetime but according to tradition when her body was exhumed from its simple grave in Dereham churchyard in

---

*History and Antiquities of Ely. James Bentham.

order for it to be transferred to the church a spring of clear water emerged from the place where her body had rested. A chapel was built around the well and for centuries to come it was a popular place of pilgrimage especially for those seeking cures for their sicknesses as the water was reputed to possess miraculous healing powers. Visitors to Dereham will find Withburga's well in the graveyard of the parish church. The inscription above it describes how the abbot and monks of Ely stole her relics and translated them to their own monastery where in the church they were interred near the relics of her sisters, Etheldreda and Sexburg.

Ely minster had been destroyed by Danish invaders in 870. A number of entries in the *Anglo-Saxon Chronicle* indicate that the monasteries were a special target for the Danish attackers. We read for instance in the Laud Manuscript that in 870 "the host went across Mercia into East Anglia. . . the Danes won the victory and slew the king (Edmund) and overran the entire kingdom and destroyed all the monasteries to which they came. . . they came to the monastery of Medeshamstede (Peterborough) and burned and demolished it, and slew the abbot and monks. . ." It was not because they were strongly opposed to Christianity that the Danes destroyed the monasteries; on the contrary they readily accepted the religion themselves once they had settled on English soil; it was because the monasteries were the storehouses of great wealth and treasure and the possessors of valuable estates and property that they were attacked and plundered.

The destruction of the monasteries, the loss of their treasures and manuscripts, the murder or dispersal of their monks led to an almost complete end of monastic life in England and because the monasteries had been the power-houses of learning and culture a decline in these followed too. But the monastic ideal was to revive once more in the second half of the tenth century in the reign of King Edgar under the inspiration of Dunstan, archbishop of Canterbury, Aethelwold, bishop of Winchester and Oswald, bishop of Worcester. In about 964 a new abbey was founded at Ramsey in the East Anglian fens and the two other great fenland minsters, Peterborough and Ely, were restored in 966 and 970 respectively. With the recovery of monastic life came a revival of learning and a renewed production of books in the scriptoria of the monasteries. The Benedictine Rule was once more observed and this was translated into English by Bishop Aethelwold. The relics of the saints, if indeed they were the true relics, had survived the Danish destruction of the monastic churches for they had been securely encased in stone coffins and shrines, and once these had been despoiled of their treasure they were of little value to the Danish plunderers. The relics, genuine or spurious, were at the time of the monastic revival once more sacredly enshrined and given a place of honour in the new monastic churches.

The translation of Withburga's relics took place in 974, when Brythnoth was abbot of Ely, which was one of the first monasteries to be restored after the Danish invasions. The removal and transference of relics from one place to another was common at this time when newly restored monasteries wished to enhance the reputation of their establishments as worthy centres of pilgrimage, for the greater the number of pilgrims who visited a shrine the greater was the financial benefit to the abbey concerned. Abbot Brythnoth was no exception. He openly gained the permission of King Edgar to transfer Withburga's remains from Dereham to Ely but resorted to stealth and subterfuge when he perceived opposition from the men of Dereham. He and his fellow monks, after giving a feast to the clergy and notables of Dereham, stole the relics from the church while their guests, satiated with rich food and wine, slept. The relics were conveyed by boat from Brandon to Ely where amidst great rejoicing they were carried in procession to the monastic church and enshrined beside the relics of the two other royal princesses. All attempts of the men of Dereham to recover their treasure failed but they still had their holy well; no thieves could deprive them of that and pilgrims in their thousands resorted to it until the time of the Reformation.

7 St Botolph and the Rule of St Benedict

NEAR to the estuary of the river Alde in Suffolk stands a secluded little fourteenth century church dedicated to St Botolph and belonging to the village of Iken; it was most likely the site of a monastery, built by Botolph in the middle of the seventh century. The natural aspect of the place certainly accords with the description of the site, given by Folcard, the saint's biographer, writing in 1068 when he was abbot of Thorney in Cambridgeshire. The place, he says, is one of "dismal swamps, surrounded on all by the branches of a river."

It is unfortunate that few reliable historical facts exist in connection with Botolph, for his popularity in Anglo-Saxon and medieval times was widespread and his influence on the religious life of eastern England and beyond, obviously strong. Bede makes no reference to him though it is certain that he knew of him. The *Anglo-Saxon Chronicle* records the founding of his monastery in 654: "In this year King Anna was killed; and Botwulf began to build a monastery at Icanhoh." Another reference to him occurs in an early eighth century work known as the *Life of Ceolfrith*. The writer, a monk of Jarrow where Ceolfrith was abbot, tells how at the age of twenty-seven Ceolfrith was ordained to the priesthood by Bishop Wilfrid at Ripon. Wilfrid, a staunch upholder of the discipline and practice of the Roman Church, had introduced into the northern monasteries the Rule of St Benedict and had no doubt inspired his young disciple Ceolfrith with an equal enthusiasm for the Rule. Soon after his ordination in 669 Ceolfrith visited Canterbury to study the Benedictine, and other monastic rules. After a period of residence and tuition at the famous monastery of St Peter and St Paul where Theodore, the recently appointed archbishop of Canterbury had just arrived, Ceolfrith returned to his monastery at Ripon. His route northwards took him through the province of East Anglia where Botolph, renowned for his knowledge of monasticism, had his own monastery at Icanhoh. Ceolfrith stayed with Botolph as long as time would allow and learned from him a wealth of information on religious matters. In the work to which we refer, Botolph is described as "a man of unparalleled life and learning, and full of the grace of the Holy Spirit."* This early reference to his monastery in East Anglia must be regarded as primary evidence for its existence at either Iken in Suffolk or at some other place in East Anglian territory, rather than at Boston on the river Witham in Lincolnshire which some have claimed to be the original site of his monastery. There is likely however to be a good reason for the tradition which connects Boston with the saint. According to a *Life of Botolph* in an eleventh century German breviary he made a number of journeys from Icanhoh; it is possible that he visited the district where Boston now stands, leaving a lasting impression upon the place, but this is no more than conjecture.

In a paper entitled *St Botolph and Iken,* the fruit of a great deal of research, F. S. Stevenson advances a view, which he shares with a number of other scholars, that Icanhoh is to be identified with Iken in Suffolk and not with Boston in Lincolnshire.† In support of his view he refers, among other things, to the *Ely Chronicle* which states that Botolph built his monastery during the reign of Ethelhere of East Anglia. Mr Stevenson points out that Ethelhere's territory did not reach as far north as Boston and he could not therefore have made a grant of land to Botolph at Boston. The *Anglo-Saxon Chronicle* corroborates the piece of chronology that the monastery was built in the year King Anna died, 654. Anna was then succeeded by his brother Ethelhere. We may surmise that it was Anna, a devout Christian, who made the grant of land to Botolph and that Botolph built his monastery during the reign of Ethelhere, having perhaps begun it while Anna was still alive.

Folcard, writing his biography almost four hundred years after Botolph's death and on the occasion of the saint's relics being brought to Thorney Abbey, introduces some strange names into his account of the saint's life. He tells how Botolph was given land and permission to build a monastery by "Ethelmund king of the Southern Angles." He was urged to make this grant by his kinsmen, Adelhere and Adelwold and by his sisters. Folcard, who was not an Englishman, may have been confusing the names of East Anglia's kings, for no record of a seventh century King Ethelmund survives. The names Adelhere and Adelwold are

---

*English Historical Documents. Volume I. Number 155.

†Proceedings. Suffolk Institute of Archaeology. XVIII. 1922.

reminiscent of the two brothers of Anna, Ethelhere and Ethelwald who in turn became kings of East Anglia. If Folcard was writing of King Anna and wrongly calling him Ethelmund he might equally wrongly have been calling the two women, sisters, instead of daughters of the king. As we have seen, Anna's daughters were all connected in some way with monastic life and would certainly have favoured the establishment of a monastery such as Botolph's in East Anglia. But it is of course possible that Folcard was writing of a king or sub-king named Ethelmund who is otherwise unknown.*

In the eleventh century German breviary, Botolph is referred to as an Irishman, but Folcard speaks of him as a Saxon, who with his brother went to the Continent to learn the principles of monastic life and then returned to eastern England where the king gave him land to found a monastery. If we are right in thinking that the monastery was built at Iken in Suffolk then it would have been only a short distance from the royal court at Rendlesham and not far from Dommoc the seat of the East Anglian bishop.

Like Guthlac's secluded hermitage at Crowland, Botolph's chosen retreat was haunted by demons, but when the saint approached the place they were unable to endure the presence of so holy a man and "with loud wailings they quitted the place." Such references to demons are common in the early *Lives of the Saints* and can be interpreted in a variety of ways. Perhaps they are best seen as attempts by writers to give concrete expression to the forces of evil with which the saints had to contend and to demonstrate their power to overcome them. Like Christ himself, who grappled with Satan in the wilderness, the saints were committed to a perpetual war against evil. As well as featuring in ancient Christian literature demons were commonly depicted in medieval times in various art forms: in illuminated manuscripts and in ecclesiastical imagery, in stained glass, wall paintings, stone carvings and so on. Many examples of such portrayals survive in our English churches and most likely derive their origin from these early literary sources.

When Botolph had expelled the demons from the place where he intended to live he began to build his monastery. Unlike Guthlac of Crowland he had no wish to live the solitary life of a religious hermit and soon he was attracting other devout souls who wished

---

*The reader should be warned that some scholars regard the biography as historically worthless.

to learn from him and to emulate his holy life. It was said of Botolph that he demonstrated by his example what he preached with his mouth. He ruled his monastery as abbot, teaching and observing the Benedictine Rule. The German breviary refers to a journey he made to the Thames bank where he founded a church and dedicated it to St Martin. According to Folcard's *Life of the Saint,* he died at Icanhoh in 680 and was buried at his own monastery, but his body was also said to have rested for a time at Grundisburgh near to Iken and later at Bury St Edmunds. In the tenth century during King Edgar's reign the saint's body was reputed to have been dismembered, the various portions being distributed, by order of the king, to the abbeys at Ely and Thorney and a portion of it went to the king himself; this portion was eventually bestowed upon Westminster Abbey by Edward the Confessor. Thorney Abbey, where part of the saint's relics were enshrined, honoured his name by incorporating it into the dedication of the monastic church. To this day the parish church of Thorney, which is part of the old abbey church, bears the dedication to St Mary and St Botolph.

If the number of churches dedicated to a particular saint is indicative of the esteem with which he or she was regarded by medieval churchmen then Botolph must surely have been one of England's most popular saints. Well over sixty churches, the majority in eastern England, are dedicated to him and a number of towns and villages are also named after him.* In London at four of the city's gates, Aldgate, Bishopsgate, Billingsgate and Aldersgate, churches were built and dedicated to St Botolph suggesting that they marked the stopping places for the procession through London on the occasion of the conveyance of the sacred relics to Westminster. The eleventh century priory of St Botolph at Colchester, of which considerable ruins still remain, was built on the site of an earlier Saxon church, also dedicated to the saint. But the most impressive church in eastern England bearing the name of St Botolph is that at Boston in the Lincolnshire fens, its immensely tall tower standing out as a landmark for miles around and visible from Hunstanton on the other side of the Wash. On the south side of the church's tower, on one of its parapets, the stone work now much eroded through exposure to the weather, is the carved figure of Botolph overlooking the town, his hand raised in blessing. Other representations of him appear in various churches.

Studies in Church Dedications. F. Arnold-Forster.

In the north aisle of Wiggenhall St Mary Magdalene in Norfolk he is seen among a fine collection of fifteenth century stained glass figures, dressed as a bishop with crozier and mitre.

The fame of Botolph was not confined to eastern England for we find him connected with a religious establishment in Shropshire. In the last quarter of the seventh century, around the year 680, a double minster was founded at Much Wenlock. An early charter, believed to be genuine, reveals its connections with the monastery at Icanhoh. Much Wenlock was either founded by Mildburg or she became abbess shortly after its foundation. She was the daughter of Merewalh, king of the Magonsaetan people on the Welsh border. Merewalh had married a woman of the royal house of Kent, Domneva, later abbess of the minster in Thanet. She was succeeded there as abbess by her daughter Mildred who had been trained in religion at Chelles near Paris. But it is Mildred's sister Mildburgh who concerns us here. In his *Life of Mildburg* the monk Goscelin writing in the eleventh century incorporates into his work "an autobiographical statement, professedly drawn up or dictated by Mildburg herself."* In it she refers to five charters relating to estates she had received from various benefactors, one of them being from Edelheg, abbot of Icanhoh. He writes, "In the name of my Lord Jesus Christ, I Edelheg, Abbot of the monastery called Icheanog, with the consent of the whole household of Abbot Botulph of holy memory, give to the consecrated virgin Mildburg an estate of ninety seven hides in the place called Wimnicas (Much Wenlock) . . .But on condition that the aforesaid place shall by grace of God remain unalterably under the tutelage of the church of the worshipful Abbot Botolph, not under compulsion but of its own accord, since it is with the money of that same church that the land is being purchased from the king named Merwald."

The charter thus shows the minster at Wenlock to be a daughter house of St Botolph's monastery at Icanhoh founded twenty-six years after the founding of Icanhoh. It shows too that St Boltoph's monastery during those years must have increased in importance and acquired considerable wealth in order to be in a position to make such a donation to the Abbess Mildburg.

It seems strange perhaps that a monastic house in East Anglia should be taking an interest in one so far away in the West Midlands, but this was no doubt due to contacts existing between members

*The Early Charters of the West Midlands. H. P. R. Finberg.

of the two communities. The close tie that existed between the monasteries and the royal families not only brought the monks into contact with kings, princes, princesses and noblemen of the kingdom in which their own monasteries had been founded but also with the royalty of other kingdoms. As we have seen the royal house of East Anglia was connected, by the marriage of some of its members, to the royal house of Kent and Kent in turn was connected with the Magonsaetan kingdom in the West Midlands by the marriage of Domneva and Merewalh. Botolph, an authority on monastic life, had most likely visited the Kentish minsters and met their abbesses including Domneva at Thanet and her daughters Mildred and Mildburg. Nor must we leave out of account the Frankish minsters, which, as H. P. R. Finberg points out, were having a strong influence on English monastic life at that time. Mildred had received her training at Chelles in France and three of King Anna's progeny, his daughter Ethelberga, his step-daughter Saethryth and his grand-daughter Earcongota were in turn abbesses of the double minster at Faremoutier-en-Brie, near Meaux. Botolph had most likely learned the principles of monastic life at one or other of these minsters and had come into contact there with the English abbesses. It is not surprising then that he and his brethren should have taken steps to encourage members of the English royal families to foster the development of the religious life in other parts of Britain. Although the grant of land was not made to Mildburg until shortly after Botolph's death we may surmise that plans for such a transaction were made during his life time.

The Rule of St Benedict

Among the monastic rules which Ceolfrith went to Canterbury and Icanhoh to study was that of St Benedict, which was later to be introduced into the twin monasteries of Monkwearmouth and Jarrow where Ceolfrith was abbot. This rule, of which St Botolph possessed an expert knowledge, was observed, though not exclusively, in the English minsters of the seventh century and in the tenth century reform movement it was reintroduced into the restored monasteries by Aethelwold, bishop of Winchester. In later centuries Benedict was to give his name to countless monasteries all over the world where his rule was observed.

Benedict was born in about 480 in Nursia in central Italy. Pope Gregory the Great, who wrote an account of his life, tells how as a youth he was sent to Rome for his education but was disturbed to find that secular studies and worldly knowledge led many of his fellow students into evil ways. He, being of a devout nature and wishing only to serve God, abandoned his studies, turned his back on Rome and went in search of a secluded place where he might devote his mind to divine contemplation. He found such a place in a mountain cave at Subiaco, forty miles or so from Rome. For three years he stayed there, praying and fasting and, like John the Baptist, clothing himself in the skins of animals which aroused the curiosity of some passing shepherds who spied him through the bushes and "verily thought that he had been some beast."* But when they found that he was a man of God they often came to talk with him and to nourish their souls with his wisdom; and they in return brought him food to sustain his body.

The fame of Benedict spread to all the region around Subiaco and many came to receive counsel from him for, as his name implies, there was goodness in all his words. Monks from a nearby monastery, whose abbot had recently died, came to implore him to come to their monastery to rule them as their new abbot. Reluctantly Benedict agreed to their proposal and left his quiet hermitage to govern the monks; but they very soon regretted their choice of a new abbot for they had grown slack and accustomed to soft living and Benedict's regime was too strict for them. Because of this, they began to hate him and, if a miracle had not intervened to save him, they would have poisoned him. With a prayer on his lips for their forgiveness and charging them to look for an abbot after their own heart he returned to the solace of his mountain grotto. But once again disciples gathered around him, desiring to be taught by him, and when he saw that they were truly in earnest he allowed them to build a small monastery near to his cave. This was the first of twelve monasteries in the district, each one housing twelve monks and an abbot, Benedict being the Director of them all. Here, in the region of Subiaco, Benedict remained for a number of years, supervising the monks' training, educating the boys who were sent to him from Rome and accumulating for himself an ever increasing knowledge of Christian living and monastic discipline, all of which was to serve him for what lay ahead.

In 529 and approaching fifty, Benedict, with the well-being of his monastic sons at heart, left Subiaco and with a small group of

---

*The Dialogues of Gregory. Edited by E. G. Gardner.

disciples travelled southwards to the town of Casinum at the foot of the great hill, known now as Monte Cassino, half-way between Rome and Naples. On this glorious hill-top site, where once had stood a pagan temple of Jupiter, Benedict and his monks built a monastery, living in obedience to religious discipline and preaching the Gospel to the peasants in the area. It was here at Monte Cassino, where he stayed until his death in 547, that Benedict drew up for his monks the "little Rule for beginners" which was destined to find its way into innumerable monasteries and nunneries all over the world and throughout the centuries that were to follow. The Rule, which shows the influence of other standard rules in use at the time, particularly that of the anonymous Rule of the Master and the eastern Rule of St Basil, was the culminating achievement of a lifetime of personal devotion, intellectual study and wide experience of monastic life in its various aspects. Intended only to serve his small community at Monte Cassino, Benedict's Rule was to become and remains to this day "the monastic code par excellence in the Western Church."*

To the ordinary Christian layman the most striking feature of the Rule is the breadth of its application, for although it was compiled for monks living under vows of poverty, chastity and obedience, and much of it is relevant only to those living within such a framework, yet it contains a great deal of material which is applicable to Christians in general whatever their secular calling. It displays qualities of humanity, moderation, reasonableness and practicality which give it an appeal far beyond the cloister, and its language possesses a beauty and simplicity which has power to touch the heart and to inspire the mind. Here, for instance, is a piece of advice which cannot be said to apply only to monks.

"Whatever good work thou undertakest, ask him with most instant prayer to perfect it, so that he who has deigned to count us among his sons may never be provoked by our evil conduct. For we must always so serve him with the gifts that he has given us."†

And here, the monk is directed to perform acts of mercy towards his neighbour.

Saints and Scholars. David Knowles.

† *The Rule of St Benedict*. Translated Justin McCann. All quotations are from this translation.

He is "To relieve the poor.
To clothe the naked.
To visit the sick.
To bury the dead.
To help the afflicted.
To console the sorrowing.
To avoid worldly conduct.
To prefer nothing to the love of Christ. . .
To reverence the old.
To love the young.
To pray for one's enemies in the love of Christ.
To make peace with one's adversary before sundown.
And never to despair of God's mercy."

The perfection to which the monk aspired was to be sought through obedience to the two great commandments of the Gospel: to love God with the whole being and to love one's neighbour as oneself. Obedience to the first commandment found its expression and fulfilment in the monk's participation in the monastic services of worship, known as the Divine Office which took precedence over all else in the daily routine. "Seven times a day have I given praise to thee," said the psalmist and seven times a day the monks assembled in the Oratory for the Offices of Lauds, Prime, Terce, Sext, None, Vespers, Compline, and the Night Office of Vigils. The psalms formed the chief component of the Offices and these were arranged so that the whole of the psalter, with its hundred and fifty psalms, was recited every week. St Benedict, in his Rule, called the Divine Office, the Opus Dei, the Work of God, and around it all other activities of the monastery revolved. It gave to the entire structure of monastic life, cohesion, meaning and purpose, for the chief aim of the monk's life was to glorify God. "As soon as the signal for the Divine Office has been heard, let them abandon what they have in hand and assemble with the greatest speed. . . Let nothing, therefore, be put before the Work of God."

In view of its central importance it is not surprising that almost a quarter of the Rule should have been devoted to regulations concerning the composition and saying of the Offices. Slovenly performance of them incurred severe censure. Anyone making a careless mistake in reciting a psalm, response, antiphon or lesson must make humble acknowledgement and apology before all present and "boys for such a fault shall be whipped." The monks are exhorted to believe, with absolute certainty, that God is present when they are performing the Divine Office. "Let us then consider how we ought to behave ourselves in the presence of God and his angels, and so sing the psalms, that mind and voice may be in harmony." Bede, the monk and scholar of Jarrow monastery, where the Benedictine Rule was certainly known and probably observed, though perhaps not in its entirety, most likely had this chapter of the Rule in mind when he said "I know that the angels are present at the Canonical Hours, and what if they do not find me among the brethren when they assemble? Will they not say, Where is Bede? Why does he not attend the appointed devotions with his brethren?"*

Love for his neighbour was the second duty of the monk. He was to submit himself in obedience, not only to his superiors, but also to his fellow monks, showing more concern for the good of others than for his own and bearing with the greatest patience the infirmities and weaknesses of others. Consideration was to be shown to the children and aged monks in the community and for them the rules regarding food and drink could be slackened. Above all, "care must be taken of the sick, so that they may be served in very deed as Christ himself; for he said: I was sick and ye visited me; and, what ye did to one of these least ones, ye did unto me." But this command to tend the sick for Christ's sake was balanced by a word of warning to the sick themselves. They were to show consideration for those who tended them and to refrain from making unreasonable demands.

To the ordinary Christian of today, living outside of the cloister and accustomed to the comforts and luxuries of modern life, the Rule of St Benedict may seem strict, even austere, but compared to other monastic rules of his time, particularly the Celtic rule of Columbanus, to which we have referred, and the rules of the eastern Church, it was mild and humane. It laid no special emphasis on asceticism and penitential practices such as we find in the Rule of Columbanus. It asked of the brethren "nothing that is harsh or burdensome." Corporal punishment was not excluded from the Rule but unlike Columbanus' Rule which prescribed it for minor offences, "twelve blows for uttering an idle word" and such like, Benedict's Rule recommended the rod only for serious offences and repeated failure to respond to correction. Delinquent boys too were to be punished "with severe fasts or chastised with sharp stripes, in order that they may be cured."

---

*Bede. Sherley-Price. Introduction.

The number of hours, more in winter than summer, allotted to sleep, was sufficient for the maintenance of the brethrens' health and efficiency. A light burned all night in the dormitory and the monks slept fully clothed so that there should be no delay when the signal went for the Night Office of Matins. The gentle injunction, with which the chapter on sleep ends, shows Benedict's tolerant understanding of human frailty. "When they rise for the Work of God, let them gently encourage one another, on account of the excuses to which the sleepy are addicted."

The amount of food provided for the brethren at the daily meal was to be sufficient and varied enough to promote their health; "gluttony must be avoided, so that a monk never be surprised by a surfeit." Except during sickness the diet excluded meat but not poultry and fish. A choice of two main dishes was offered, to allow for peculiarities of digestion and taste " so that he who perchance cannot eat the one, may make his meal of the other," and in addition, when they were available, a third dish of young vegetables or fruit, could be provided. Monks engaged in heavy work were to be allowed an extra amount of bread and the young were to receive smaller portions than their elders. Silence was to be observed during the meal so that all could attend to the words of the reader. The brethren were to be alert to supply each others' needs at the table, but if a need happened to go unnoticed the monk was to make it known by a sign and not by words.

Though Benedict himself maintained that wine was an unsuitable drink for monks, no doubt because of its intoxicating properties, the monks were unconvinced of this and it remained their principal beverage. But, says the Rule, "let us at least agree upon this, to drink temperately and not to satiety: *for wine maketh even the wise to fall away.*" And if the circumstances of the locality in which the monks lived caused the ration of wine to be reduced or even stopped altogether, "then let the monks who dwell there bless God and not murmur."

The clothes of the brethren had to be suitable to the climate of the locality: thick and woolly in cold climates and in wintertime, thin in summer and in warm climates. A monk was to have two tunics and cowls "to allow for a change at night and for the washing of these garments," and they must fit well "that they be not too short for the wearers." Worn out clothes were not to be discarded but kept in the storeroom, to be given to the poor. Extra underclothing was provided for monks who went on journeys; these garments were to be washed and put back in the storeroom when the monk returned; he was also given a more respectable tunic and cowl to wear while he was away.

For the Benedictine monk, manual labour possessed a dignity and value unknown in the pagan world of the Roman Empire in which menial tasks were performed predominately by slaves. "Idleness is the enemy of the soul" stated the Rule, "The brethren, therefore, must be occupied at stated hours in manual labour, and again at other hours in sacred reading." Although the sick and the weak were to be given special consideration, they too were to busy themselves with some craft or other employment "so that they be not idle." For the vigorous and healthy brethren there were a variety of tasks to be performed, upon which the survival and stability of the community depended. There was work to be done in the monastery itself, in the kitchen, where every monk took his turn, in the refectory, the bakehouse, the storerooms, the guest house and so on. There was outdoor work to be done in the gardens, fields, orchards, farms and vineyards, and if the heavy work of harvesting was to be done by the brethren they must not do it in a spirit of discontent. Those monks who were gifted at some particular craft or artistic skill were to be allowed, subject to the abbot's permission, to practise it, but they must do so in the spirit of humility, not imagining that they were bestowing a great benefit upon the community. If the goods they produced were to be sold, the prices were to be kept low, "a little cheaper than they are sold by people of the world."

In a community such as that at Monte Cassino the importance of leadership is recognised. The Rule specifies what kind of man the abbot of a monastery is to be. "Let him study rather to be loved than feared." He is to hate all kinds of wrong-doing in his sons but his love for them must not cease and in his attempts to correct their faults he must exercise moderation, prudence and charity, avoiding excessive harshness "lest being too zealous in removing the rust he break the vessel." He must behave towards them with the loving-kindness of a father and the solicitude of a shepherd, admonishing, encouraging, exhorting and rebuking. Particular care and concern was to be shown towards erring brethren, and, like the Good Shepherd of the Gospel, the abbot of the monastery was to take great pains and employ every possible means to recover the one who had strayed "so that he may not lose any of the sheep entrusted to him." As to the abbot's own life and conduct, he should be "learned in the divine law. . . . chaste, sober, and merciful" instructing his sons more by his example than by his words, and let him understand that he who teaches the Rule to others must first observe it himself.

In the final chapter, St Benedict modestly claims that the observance of his Rule ought to produce in those who follow it some degree of virtue, and a rudimentary knowledge of monastic discipline. But for those who would reach to the heights of perfection there were the teachings of the Fathers, the writings of the Old and New Testaments, the Conferences and Institutes of Cassian and the Rule of the holy Father Basil. "Whoever therefore, thou art that hasteneth to thy heavenly country, fulfil first of all by the help of Christ this little Rule for beginners. And then at length, under God's protection, shalt thou attain those aforesaid loftier heights of wisdom and virtue."

In view of the importance of the Rule of St Benedict it is not surprising that a number of manuscripts have survived, the earliest being in the possession of the Bodleian Library. This copy of the Rule is written in a beautifully clear uncial script which paleographers assign to the beginning or middle of the eighth century.* It has been suggested that it may have been written for Bishop Wilfrid of York, a celebrated Churchman of the late seventh and early eighth centuries who as we have seen was a champion of Roman Christianity in England and was responsible for introducing the Rule into the monasteries of Mercia and Northumbria. But, as Dr Farmer points out, if the manuscript is assigned to the middle of the eighth century it cannot have had Wilfrid as its patron for he died in 709.

It should have become apparent from the last four chapters that by the end of the seventh century Christianity had made remarkable progress in East Anglia and that the kingdom had become rich in monastic establishments which functioned as centres of piety and learning and of Christian evangelism in the different areas of the kingdom. In the eastern, coastal regions there was Felix's minster and bishop's seat at Dunwich or Felixstowe, Botolph's famous monastery at Icanhoh and Fursey's

---

*The Rule of St Benedict. Early English Manuscript in Facsimile. Edited by D. H. Farmer.

(xvi)   St Felix and St Furseus (Fursey) detail from fifteenth century stained glass, Blythburgh Church, Suffolk.   *Parker and Jenkins, Southwold, and Ipswich Museum*

(xvii)   Ruined church of St Felix, Babingly, Norfolk.   *Margaret Gallyon*

(xix) St Etheldreda. Fifteenth century stained glass. Sandringham Church, Norfolk.

Royal Commission on Historic Monuments

(xviii) St Withburga. Nineteenth century stained glass, Fritton Church, Suffolk.

Margaret Gallyon

(xx)   Top. Etheldreda's marriage to Egfid. Bottom. Etheldreda installed as abbess of Ely by Bishop
Wilfrid. Octagon Capitals, Ely Cathedral.   *Rev. Maurice Ridgway*

(xxi)   Ely Cathedral today.   *Margaret Gallyon*

(xxii)   Church of St Withburga, Holkham, Norfolk.
                            Margaret Gallyon by kind permission of Lord Leicester

The Ruins of a Tomb which contained the Remains of
WITHBURGA
youngest Daughter of
ANNAS
King of the East Angles
who died A.D. 654
The Abbot and Monks of Ely
stole this precious Relique
and translated it to Ely Cathedral
where it was interred near her three Royal Sisters
A.D. 974

xxiii)   Withburga's well, Dereham Churchyard, Norfolk.   *Margaret Gallyon*

xxiv)   Medieval Pilgrim Badges depicting a) The Holy House of Walsingham b) St Thomas of Canterbury c) and d) St Etheldreda and e) St Alban.   *London Museum*

a

b

c

d

e

f

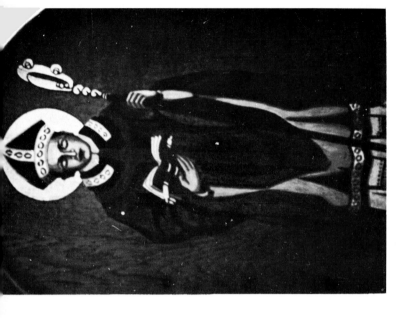

(xxvi) Representation of St Cedd, West Mersea Church, Essex. *Margaret Gallyon*

(xxv) St Botolph. Fifteenth century stained glass, St Mary Magdalene, Wiggenhall, Norfolk. *R. W. Stannard*

(xxvii)   Ancient print of Crowland Abbey.

(xxviii)   Church of St Peter-ad-Murum, Bradwell-on-Sea, Essex. Probably built by St Cedd in
the seventh century.   *Jan Wise*

(xxx) Roundel from the Guthlac Roll depicting Guthlac appearing in a vision to King Aethelbald. *British Museum*

(xxix) Roundel from the Guthlac Roll depicts St Bartholomew and an angel talking with Guthlac. *British Museum*

Celtic monastery at Burgh Castle though we do not know how long this survived after Fursey's departure to France. In the western area of the kingdom there was Etheldreda's double minster at Ely, and monasteries, probably at Soham and Bury St Edmunds; in the north was a second bishop's seat and most likely a minster at Elmham and five miles or so away Withburga's small house of nuns. We may attribute this flowering of religious devotion in East Anglia not only to the enterprise and zeal of the missionaries but also to the enthusiasm of the rulers and in particular the kings Sigbert and Anna, who supported the clergy in their efforts to spread the Faith.

8 St Cedd and the Conversion of Essex

THE kingdom of the East Saxons, now Essex, lay sandwiched between East Anglia to the north and Kent to the south and extended beyond the present day boundaries, incorporating, as well as Essex, parts of Hertfordshire and almost the whole of Middlesex and Surrey. It was a flat, thickly forested region flanked to the north and south by the rivers Stour and Thames. The great belt of forest stretched from the Chilterns in the west to the Essex coast in the east and at its widest was forty miles across; a section of the forest still survives in the Epping area. Except where Roman bricks and masonry remained and could be re-used, buildings were made of timber, for stone was scarce in the province. Even today timber spires are a distinctive feature of Essex churches, but the only surviving timber church of later Saxon times is at Greenstead, its nave being made of vertically split oak trunks. The church claims to have been the temporary resting place for St Edmund's body while it was being transferred from Bury St Edmunds to London.

In the first half of the seventh century the chief city of the East Saxon kingdom was London but later it came under Mercian control. It had been of major political and commercial importance in Roman times and in AD 314 sent its bishop to the Council of Arles. Bede describes it as "a trading centre for many nations who visit it by land and sea." Pope Gregory had originally intended that it should be Augustine's metropolitan city and centre of his mission to the English, but after the initial success at Canterbury no transfer to London was possible, for the kingdom of Essex was at that time subordinate to that of Kent. London, however, by 604, was a centre of evangelism among the East Saxon people and the seat of a bishopric.

Paganism was deeply rooted in Essex whose rulers claimed descent from their ancestral god Saxnot. Even after their conversion to Christianity we hear of frequent relapses into paganism and a return to the worship of idols. The first attempts to convert their people came when Augustine in 604 consecrated Mellitus to be their bishop, with London as his cathedral city. Mellitus had come to England with the second group of missionaries whom Pope Gregory sent in 601, so before becoming bishop of London he had had three years experience of working among the pagan English. Support and encouragement in his mission to the East Saxons came from King Ethelbert of Kent who was uncle to the reigning king, Sabert. He built and endowed a cathedral church in London probably on the site of an ancient Roman temple, dedicated to Diana. Ethelbert's church was dedicated to the Apostle Paul and almost certainly on the same site today stands London's great cathedral church of St Paul's. But Mellitus's seventh century church would have been a small and simple structure with nave, semi-circular apse and a chapel or porticus on either side, in the style of the Kentish churches.

King Sabert, perhaps due to pressure from his overlord, accepted the new religion and was baptized, encouraging Mellitus in the task of converting his people. When Mellitus had worked among them for five or six years we hear of him going to Rome to discuss the affairs of the English Church with the pope. While in Rome he attended a synod of Italian bishops who had gathered to formulate regulations regarding monastic discipline. On his return he was able to convey the decisions of the synod to leaders of the English Church so that they could be implemented in the monasteries. They would not apply of course to the Celtic monasteries for as yet the practices of the Celtic Church had not been brought into line with the Church of Rome.

The spread of the Faith in Essex progressed unhindered while Ethelbert and Sabert were alive but when they died in 616 and 617, respectively, a reversion to paganism occurred, for Sabert's three sons, who became joint rulers of the kingdom, were obdurate pagans. While their father had been alive they had deceived him into thinking that they had accepted the new religion though they had refused baptism, but after his death they openly reverted to idolatrous practises and a wave of paganism swept through the whole kingdom, threatening to obliterate the Faith which Mellitus had so energetically preached. While celebrating the Eucharist in St Paul's Church and ministering to the faithful, Mellitus was on one occasion interrupted by the rebellious rulers who demanded to receive the consecrated bread as their father Sabert had done. Mellitus explained that this was forbidden and urged them first to be baptized, "so long as you reject the water of life, you are quite unfit to receive the bread of life," he said. But the young rulers denied their need of baptism, though the bishop repeatedly told them of the Church's law on the matter. His firm adherence to the discipline of the Church and his refusal to sacrifice principle for the sake of expediency and personal advantage led to his expulsion from his bishopric and from the East Saxon kingdom. With his fellow clergy he came to Kent to discuss his next move with Laurence, the archbishop and with Justus, bishop of Rochester.

Laurence too was undergoing great trials and disappointments in Kent, where King Eadbald, son and successor of Ethelbert, was encouraging a return to paganism and had himself violated the Church's marriage law by marrying his own stepmother. Besides this, Eadbald suffered from attacks of mental derangement, caused, it was said, by his immoral ways. After discussing the present and unstable state of affairs in the English kingdoms the three bishops decided that rather than stay among a rebellious and stubborn race who had rejected the Word of Life they would do better to return to Rome where they could be more profitably occupied. We would be unwise to judge their decision as a cowardly one in which they showed themselves ready to retreat in face of difficulty, for it is certain that after careful consideration they agreed that this was the right course to take. Christ had uttered a stern denunciation of those cities and villages which rejected the Gospel, declaring that the notoriously evil cities of Sodom and Gomorrha would be shown more leniency in the day of judgement than they.* His disciples were, he said, to leave such places and to shake the dust from their feet.

In 617 Mellitus and Justus left for France and if Laurence had not, while engaged in fervent prayer for the Church, received a vision of St Peter, he too would have followed them. But, as we have seen, Eadbald repented of his former wickedness when he heard of the archbishop's vision and he then accepted the new Faith, giving up his unlawful wife and encouraging the spread of Christianity in his kingdom. He recalled Justus and Mellitus from France, Justus being restored to Rochester and Mellitus to Kent, for although the three pagan sons of Sabert had been killed in battle, the people of Essex still preferred their pagan priests and refused to have Mellitus back in London.

---

*Matthew, chapter 10, verse 15.

After the death of Archbishop Laurence in 619 Mellitus succeeded him to Canterbury, but he ruled the English Church for no longer than five years for he was in poor health and crippled with gout, though his mind remained clear and energetic to the end. He died in 624 and his body was laid to rest beside his two predecessors in the monastic church of St Peter and St Paul. It was now the turn of Justus to succeed to the archbishopric of Canterbury.

Thirty years elapsed before a second attempt was made to convert Essex, this time by Celtic missionaries. The political scene had taken a turn for the better and the kingdom was ably ruled now by Sigbert the Good, not to be confused with East Anglia's learned king of the same name. Sigbert of Essex had been persuaded by his friend King Oswy of Northumbria that the God of the Christians was more worthy of worship than the gods of their pagan forefathers. But the question as to whether Essex should accept the new religion was not merely a matter of the king's own personal decision, it concerned his court, his thanes and all his people so he summoned his witan to discuss the matter. A decision was reached that Christianity should become the official religion of the kingdom. The king with members of his court and council were the first to receive baptism from Bishop Finan of Lindisfarne. Next it was necessary to find teachers to expound the Faith to the general population and for this purpose Oswy found teachers from among the Celtic Christians. There was an Englishman named Cedd, who had been a pupil of the saintly monk Aidan, and was at that time preaching in the kingdom of Middle Anglia. Oswy recalled Cedd from his work there and, with one other priest to help him, sent him to Essex. The two men conducted a preliminary preaching tour all over the kingdom, baptizing some and establishing small Christian communities in scattered areas. The date was about 653 and for the next eleven years Cedd was to minster to these unlearned peasants of Essex.

After the success of his first preaching tour Cedd returned to Lindisfarne to report on his work to Bishop Finan who decided to promote him to the rank of bishop so that he could ordain priests and deacons to help him in the task of evangelizing the East Saxons. Bede tells us that he built churches in several places in Essex, one in the "city which the Saxons called Ythancaestir". This was its old English name but in Roman times it was the site of one of the Saxon Shore forts, Othona, which guarded the estuary of the river

Blackwater. Little now remains of the fort but in 1867 when it was first excavated, the north, south and west walls were still standing so we may imagine that in Cedd's time, the mid-seventh century, extensive ruins of the fort must have existed, affording ample building material for a church and dwellings for a monastic community.* Apart from the supplies of building material the stout outer walls would have provided a ready-made rampart for the whole monastery and afforded protection from the severe weather to which the east coast is subject. This site, very near to the sea, wild and desolate, was the kind of place beloved of the Celtic monks, who, in their native Ireland or in Scotland selected remote islands or the windswept coasts as sites for their monastic cells. Cedd, though an Englishman, had been trained in the Celtic tradition and spent much of his life at Iona and Lindisfarne.

Cedd's church at Ythancaestir, now Bradwell-on-Sea, still stands and is visited every year by thousands of pilgrims and sight-seers. Only the rectangular nave survives, the walls consisting of Roman tiles and masonry. When it was built, sometime between 653 and 664 there was a semi-circular apse, the plan of which is still traceable on the ground and there were side chapels to the north and south of this apse or chancel. The church is similar in design to the Kentish churches of the period which suggests that Cedd may have employed builders and masons from that kingdom. Visitors will find nothing impressive or spectacular about the church; on the contrary, without its apse and side chapels, it resembles a barn, which it was for a time, before it was restored and reconsecrated in 1920. And yet there is a charm and simplicity about this isolated little church on the edge of the Essex salt-marshes which defies description and carries with it its own distinctive aura of peace and sanctity.

Here at Ythancaestir and at Tilbury on the Thames where Cedd also built a church, monastic discipline was observed and the new recruits were given simple instruction in the basic truths of the Christian Faith and in observance of a rule. It was a source of great delight to King Sigbert that the work of the Christian missionaries prospered in his kingdom for he too was a sincere believer and endeavoured to put into practise the precepts of the Gospel. And yet among the king's own kinsmen there were some who clung to their pagan ways, despising the discipline of the Church. One of his

---

*Anglo-Saxon Architecture. H. M. and J. Taylor.

kinsmen had entered into an unlawful marriage for which he received a stern rebuke from Bishop Cedd. He was excommunicated from the Church and a ban put upon his house, all God-fearing people instructed not to enter it or to eat at his table. But for some reason King Sigbert disregarded the bishop's command and went to dine at his kinsman's house. It so happened that as he left the house he met the bishop and in great distress and remorse the king dismounted from his horse and appealed to the bishop for pardon. Cedd, exercising his episcopal authority, touched him with his staff and replied in prophetic tones, "since you have refused to avoid the house of a man who is lost and damned, this very house will be the place of your death." The incident reveals with what reverence and respect bishops were regarded by Anglo-Saxon kings. The office of kingship was conferred by divine appointment but supreme authority belonged to God and the Church. The words of Bishop Cedd were to receive their tragic fulfilment when King Sigbert was treacherously murdered by his kinsman and a brother-conspirator in the house where he had been entertained. They gave as the reason for the murder that they despised and hated the king for his leniency towards his enemies whom he weakly forgave instead of wreaking vengeance against them according to the custom of their people.

King Sigbert was succeeded by Swidhelm who, Bede says, was baptized at Rendelsham in the neighbouring kingdom of East Anglia, because the king there, Ethelwald, was standing as his sponsor. But Swidhelm's reign was short and he was succeeded by the joint rulers, Sighere and Sebbi, Sighere being a worldly and pleasure-loving king who apostatized from the Faith and encouraged a return to paganism, Sebbi a devout king who ended his days as a monk.

During the earlier reigns of Sigbert and Swidhelm, Bishop Cedd had greatly advanced the spread of Christianity in Essex and was able from time to time to leave the monasteries there in order to visit his native Northumbria and to maintain his links with the northern Church. He was on good terms with the king of Northumbria and was given a grant of land in what is now Yorkshire for the building of a monastery. The site selected by Cedd was among some lonely and remote hills which seemed more suitable for the habitation of robbers or wild beasts than for men. It was, in Bede's time, known as Laestinge and has been identified with the now attractive village of Lastingham. In the Norman crypt of the church are a large number of Saxon carved stones and fragments of crosses which testify to the antiquity of the site as a place of Christian worship.*

In this wild and desolate spot Cedd decided to build his monastery. But first he must purge it of all evil associations and of crimes which had once been committed there. Cedd resolved to spend the whole of Lent fasting and praying in the place and preparing it for the worship of God. Every day he fasted until evening and then only took a little watered milk, a piece of bread and a hen's egg. Here too we may imagine he devoutly recited psalms and litanies and prayed earnestly for the brethren in Essex and for this new monastery at Lastingham. In 659 the monastery was built and housed with monks and new recruits, the Rule being based on that observed at Lindisfarne. He himself became its first abbot, managing its affairs while he was there, but appointing representatives to take charge while he was away in Essex. It was from the monks of Lastingham that Bede gathered his information about Bishop Cedd and his brother Chad when he was writing his *History of the English Church*. It was to this monastery too that Etheldreda's household steward, Owini, came carrying his axe and his adze to show that he intended to work and not to live idle.

We hear of Bishop Cedd's presence at the synod of Whitby in 664 where he acted as interpreter, for he was fluent both in his own native tongue, English and in the Celtic language which he had learnt at Lindisfarne and Iona. The double monastery at Whitby had been founded only two years before his own monastery at Lastingham and was not more than fifteen miles away across the moors. The synod was convened to discuss the urgent problem of the differences between Roman and Celtic customs, particularly the date of Easter which was celebrated at different times by the two branches of the Church.† The controversy was settled in favour of Roman practice and Cedd was among those who accepted the decision of the synod and returned to his Essex diocese resolved to bring the Church there into conformity with the rest of Roman Christendom.

But soon after the synod, the Church in Essex was to suffer a serious setback for Cedd caught the plague and died. The out-

---

*Anglo-Saxon Architecture. H. M. and J. Taylor.

†For an account of this important synod see Bede. III. 25.

break of 664 was a particularly severe one and swept across Europe claiming thousands of victims, and in Britain and Ireland many died of it. Cedd succumbed to the disease while he was visiting his Northumbrian monastery at Lastingham. His body was buried there, in the open at first, but later in a place of honour near the altar of the stone church. His passing caused great grief to the monks of his East Saxon monastery and thirty of them, quite regardless of the risk to their own lives travelled to Lastingham to offer their prayers and devotions at his grave. But the disease was rampant at the monastery and it was not long before all of them, except one small boy, became ill and died.

Cedd's death and that of many of his monks as well as a large number of the ordinary people caused a waning of faith in the Christian God and a return to paganism in Essex. Many had expected the new religion to safeguard them against misfortune, but when the pestilence broke out among them, the Christians caught it too and died. A return to their ancestral gods might serve, they thought, to forestall the plague's advance. So the people of Essex began once more to build shrines to Thunor, Woden and Saxnot and to revive the worship of these gods. In this, they were encouraged by one of their rulers, Sighere, the apostate. Sebbi, the other ruler, remained faithful to the new religion of Christ and urged his people to do the same. When King Wulfhere of Mercia, who had dominion over Essex, heard of Sighere's apostasy, he sent Bishop Jaruman, a man of great goodness and discretion, from his own Mercian province, to recall the king and his people to the true Faith.

After the death of Cedd the bishopric of London was held for a time by Wini who was guilty of the sin of simony for he bought the bishopric from King Wulfhere. Following him came London's most distinguished bishop of the second half of the century. He was Earconwald, who was appointed to the see in 675 by Archbishop Theodore and, according to Bede, was a man of outstanding virtue. Before his consecration to the bishopric of London he had founded two monasteries, one for men at Chertsey on the Thames and the other a double monastery for his sister Ethelburga at Barking where she was abbess. A charter survives concerning the monastery at Chertsey in which land is given to Earconwald by the sub-king of Surrey, Frithuwold.* Though Bede speaks of

---

*English Historical Documents. Volume I. Number 54.

Earconwald as having founded the monastery at Chertsey the charter indicates that there had already been one there, founded by King Egbert of Kent who, as we have seen, also founded a monastery for men at Reculver. The charter suggests that the land given to Earconwald at Chertsey was for extending the existing buildings. Perhaps for some reason Egbert's foundation had fallen into disuse and Earconwald's task was to restore and revitalize it.

It was Earconwald whom Archbishop Theodore summoned to witness the reconciliation between himself and Bishop Wilfrid of York. In Wilfrid's absence and without his knowledge Theodore had split the large Northumbrian see into three parts and appointed bishops to administer them. Years later, when Theodore was old, he was troubled by an uneasy conscience on the matter; he sent for Wilfrid and in the presence of Earconwald of London made a full confession of his unjust treatment of Wilfrid and declared his intention to restore to him all his friends, estates and property.

We know that Earconwald had some share in the formulation of a code of laws issued by the West Saxon king, Ine, who ruled from 688 to 726, for in the prologue to the laws, Ine refers to the advice and instruction he received from Haedde, bishop of Winchester and from "my bishop Earconwald".

Earconwald died in 693 after being bishop of London for eighteen years. He died at his sister's double monastery at Barking but was buried in his cathedral church of St Paul's. Bede relates that the horse-litter in which he used to be carried when he was ill was preserved by his friends and it became an object of great veneration, miracles of healing occurring in connection with it.

A charming legend associated with Earconwald has survived in a late fourteenth century poem, written when the cult of the saint was at the height of its popularity and when old St Paul's in London was a favourite centre of pilgrimage because of the relics and shrine of the saint which it contained. The poet tells how in the time of Earconwald a richly ornamented tomb was discovered in the crypt of the church during building repairs. In it was the corpse of a man, gorgeously dressed and wearing a crown. When Bishop Earconwald was summoned to the crypt he, like all the other onlookers, was mystified as to the identity of this apparently royal personage. All night he prayed most earnestly that it might be revealed to him who this kingly person was and how he came to be there. The next morning after Mass when

Earconwald led the procession to the crypt and stood by the tomb the mystery was solved for the bishop bade the corpse in Christ's name to reveal its identity. To the astonishment of everyone present the corpse spoke, saying that in life he had been neither king nor knight but a man of the legal profession. He had, he said, gained the honour and affection of all London for he judged every case with honesty and fairness. When he died the people of London mourned greatly and gave him a royal and splendid burial, but his soul could find no rest for he had died a pagan and had never received Christian baptism. Then Earconwald and the people standing by were moved with pity and wept for his pagan soul. Instantly Earconwald thought to baptize the man, "God grant thee but to live till I get water and may baptize thee in the name of the Father, the Son and the Holy Ghost," he said. But there was no need for water for the saintly bishop had let fall a tear upon the corpse which now spoke out in jubilation.

"Praised be Thou, great God and thy gracious mother,
Blessed be that blissful hour that she bore Thee,
And blessed be thou, bishop, the cure of my care. . .
The words that thou spakest and the tears of thine eyes have
become my baptism."*

Then the voice ceased and the body crumbled to dust for the soul had attained to its heavenly bliss. And when the bishop and the procession left the church all the bells of the city burst forth together to celebrate this great marvel and the wonder-working power of Earconwald, their bishop.

The double monastery at Barking in Essex, ruled by Earconwald's sister Ethelburga was founded at some time before 675, the year he was consecrated bishop of London. There was evidently a *Life of Ethelburga* in circulation in Bede's day for several times he refers to a book which was the source of his information about her. He selects certain incidents from it which he thinks will edify and interest the reader. He tells how many of the brothers there died of the plague; how Ethelburga and the whole community were shown by a heavenly light where the cemetery of the sisters was to be; how a little boy, Aesica, in the care of the sisters caught the plague and died; how shortly before Ethelburga's death one of the older sisters saw in a vision a shrouded body being drawn up to

---

*Select Early English Poems. Edited by I. Gollancz.
Also in Penguin Classics, translated by Brian Stone (1971).

heaven by golden cords which symbolized the good deeds of the abbess; and he tells, in a passage of singular beauty, how a dying sister called her attendants at mid-night and asked them to put out the lamp that burned in her room. When they disregarded her request she said, "Let the lamp burn as long as you wish: but I assure you it gives me no light. My light will come to me when dawn draws near," and so it was. The nun died at daybreak.

The Abbess Ethelburga was succeeded by Hildilid, a learned and energetic woman who governed Barking minster for many years, giving careful attention to the right observance of the monastic rule. It was to Hildilid and nine of her nuns that Aldhem, abbot of Malmesbury, dedicated his Latin prose work, *De Virginitate,* a lengthy treatise on the merits of the virgin life; it was destined to edify not only the nuns of Barking but for centuries to come it was to be a source of light and encouragement to the numerous men and women of the Religious Orders who were living under the vow of chastity. The two celebrated abbesses of Barking, Ethelburga and Hildilid, were canonized by the Church and their monastery survived until 870 when it was destroyed by Danish invaders. But a hundred years later, in King Edgar's reign, it was re-established and in medieval times it became one of the richest and most influential abbeys in England.

After Earconwald's death Waldhere became bishop of London. A letter, the earliest we possess of one Englishman to another, was written by him in about 705 to Bertwald, archbishop of Canterbury, on the question of a dispute between the kings of the East Saxons and the king of Wessex.* He asks the archbishop whether it is right for him to attend the council at Brentford which had been convened to settle the dispute, for his presence at it would mean a resumption of friendly relations with Wessex, and the Church at that time had censured the Wessex see for failing to obey certain regulations regarding the ordination of bishops. The letter shows both what a powerful influence the clergy exercised in secular affairs at the time and with what great deference the archbishops of Canterbury were regarded by the bishops under their authority.

It was from Bishop Waldhere that Sebbi, king of the East Saxons, received the religious habit towards the end of his life. He had governed the kingdom for thirty years combining his royal

---

English Historical Documents. Volume I. Number 164.

duties with devout religious practices. People said of him that he should have been a bishop instead of a king, for he was of a deeply religious nature and would have given up the throne much earlier if his wife had been willing to release him from his marriage bond. Not until they were old and the king ailing did she agree to do this. But Sebbi was not a monk for long for his sickness worsened and he died. During his last days he sent for Bishop Waldhere requesting that only he and two other attendants should be present at his passing for he feared that the great pain he might suffer towards the end would cause him to speak and act in a way unbecoming to a man of his character and position. But his fears were groundless for his end was peaceful and untroubled; at three in the afternoon he fell into a gentle sleep and breathed his last without feeling any distress or pain. Sebbi had died in his own royal city of London and was buried in St Paul's Church. He had been a great benefactor to both Church and people for he had been liberal in his almsgiving, relieving the poor and handing over to Bishop Waldhere a large sum of money to be distributed wherever there was need. By the time Sebbi died in the last decade of the century the Church, despite its earlier setbacks, had gained a firm footing in the East Saxon kingdom with Waldhere as its fifth bishop.

9   St Wilfrid and the Conversion of Sussex

SUSSEX, or the kingdom of the South Saxons, was the last of the English kingdoms to be converted to Christianity. It is perhaps surprising that it had been so little influenced by the politically precocious neighbouring kingdom of Kent with its advanced culture and early conversion to Christianity. This may be partly attributable to the geographical features of Sussex, a kingdom which was cut off from the neighbouring kingdoms to the north and east by the dense and extensive forests of Andredesweald and by wide stretches of marshland around Romney. Thus, excluded from outside influences, the South Saxon people remained pagan until the end of the seventh century. Bede, who derived his knowledge of the South Saxons from his correspondence with Daniel, bishop of Winchester, relates that an attempt had been made to preach the Faith there by some Celtic monks who had built a small monastery at Bosham near Chichester. Their abbot was Dicul, possibly that same Dicul the priest who earlier had come with Fursey to preach to the East Anglians. But Dicul and his five or six brethren made no headway in their attempts to convert the South Saxons who obstinately refused to listen to their preaching and showed no inclination to follow their way of life for most likely it seemed to them too austere and comfortless.

The discovery of a number of Roman relics at Bosham indicates that there was an important Roman settlement here and it is likely that just as Fursey and Cedd utilized Roman masonry for their monasteries at Burgh Castle and Bradwell, Dicul also constructed his monastic church of Roman materials. The present church, consisting of much of its original late Saxon architecture, is reputed to have been founded and built by King Canute in about 1020 and on the site of Dicul's earlier Celtic monastery. This beautiful coastal site, like Fursey's, is a typically Celtic one, the church standing at the head of a creek and natural harbour. Today Bosham is a popular boating centre with much of its natural charm remaining. In Dicul's day it must have been a wild and remote spot, conducive, we may imagine, to the contemplation of divine mysteries. From the undisputed evidence it can well claim to be the most ancient site of Christianity in Sussex.

The eventual conversion of Sussex was due to the missionary labours of Bishop Wilfrid of York who was, as we have seen, one of the most influential figures of seventh century England. Our knowledge of him is extensive and well attested for not only was Bede personally acquainted with him but he also received reliable information about him from Bishop Acca of Hexham who had trained under Wilfrid and had accompanied him to Rome, succeeding him as bishop of Hexham in 709. We have too a full-scale biography of Wilfrid written by his devoted disciple Eddius, the priest, in whose eyes Wilfrid was a man of heroic virtue and blameless in all the conflicts in which he was involved.* No doubt Eddius wished to portray him in a favourable light because of his personal admiration for him and because he wished to please Bishop Acca who had urged him to write the biography; the *Saints' Lives,* moreover, were intended to edify the monks and nuns who read them. But Wilfrid, like all the saints, was not without his minor flaws of character and one can discern in him a streak of arrogance and an inordinate love of worldly pomp and show. There is no doubt though that Wilfrid was a man of commanding personality and moral integrity with a sincere devotion to Christ and his Church and with a number of practical achievements to his credit.

He was born in Northumbria in 634 and at the age of fourteen entered the Celtic monastery at Lindisfarne where he came under the spell of the saintly Bishop Aidan and was greatly influenced by the emphasis there upon personal religion, ascetic discipline and simplicity of life. But a counter-influence during his formative years was to play its part in shaping his future, for at the age of nineteen he travelled to Rome to visit the shrines of the saints and to receive the blessing of the pope. At Rome and at Lyons in France he was profoundly impressed by the fine buildings, the richness and splendour of ecclesiastical ritual, the magnificent art treasures of the churches and monasteries and by the quantity of books they contained. He returned to England afire with zeal for the Roman Church and for the distinctive form of Christianity which it practised. For the rest of his life he was to champion its cause and foster its growth in England, appealing at the Council of Whitby for the adoption of its customs by the English Church.

Lives of the Saints. Translated J. F. Webb. Penguin Classics.

He built and restored churches according to the Continental pattern, furnishing them with art treasures and illuminated Gospel books and encouraging the observance of the Benedictine Rule in the monasteries. Though he was chiefly concerned with ecclesiastical affairs in the north of England we find him at various stages of his career in many parts of southern England, in Mercia, East Anglia, Middle Anglia, where for a time he had charge of the diocese, Wessex, Kent and Sussex.

His first encounter with the people of Sussex was in the year 666 when he was thirty-two years old and returning from France where, in a ceremony of great splendour, he had received episcopal consecration. The return crossing from France to England had been smooth until the ship approached the Kent coast where the crew intended to land; but without warning a south-easterly gale sprang up and tossed the ship hither and thither, driving it westwards towards the Sussex shore where it stuck fast in the sand. The native inhabitants of the province, a wild and pagan tribe of barbarians, watched the plight of the stranded vessel with eager anticipation for they reckoned that whatever was cast up upon their shores belonged to them. The men of Sussex, impatient to claim possession of the ship and its contents, swarmed round the vessel with its hundred and twenty crew and passengers including Bishop Wilfrid and his retinue. Seeing the evil intention of the Saxon tribe Wilfrid spoke peaceably to them, pleading for his mens' lives and offering them in exchange large sums of money. But money was of little interest to these uncultivated pagans; they coveted the ship, its cargo and treasure and were ready to kill any who opposed them. Their high priest and magician standing on a high mound began to curse Wilfrid and his company, endeavouring to render them powerless by his sorcery. Then, like David, the God-fearing Israelite, who with a stone slew Goliath the Philistine, one of Wilfrid's companions hurled a stone at the pagan magician who in an instant fell dead to the ground, the stone having pierced his forehead. Enraged at the death of their high priest the pagan host struck out at Wilfrid's men engaging them in a fierce battle. While his fighting men wrestled with the pagans in armed combat Wilfrid and his clergy knelt upon the shore and lifted their hands to God in prayer. Outnumbered though they were, the Christians gained the victory with a loss of only five of their men. When the battle had subsided and the pagans were preparing for renewed combat the ship's company noticed that the tide had flowed in once more and the ship was afloat. Wilfrid and his followers seizing their chance, swiftly boarded the vessel and sailed away to safety. By now the storm had abated and soon they reached the Kent coast and Sandwich harbour where they disembarked. The incident left a deep impression upon Wilfrid's mind; later he must have recalled how he had prayed upon those Saxon shores for the deliverance of his men and himself. It troubled him too that this savage tribe was still ignorant of the Christian Faith. Fifteen years were to pass before he returned to Sussex to convert them. In retrospect it must have seemed to him that his arrival in England as a newly consecrated bishop could not have been more appropriately heralded than by a storm, for from now onwards until the end of his life he was to be tossed about by the storms of ill-fortune and hounded from place to place by his enemies in Church and State.

The first blow came when he arrived in Northumbria to take up his appointment as bishop of York only to find that, because of his delay in returning from France, King Oswy had appointed another man, Chad, in his place. Chad was attached to the Celtic Church, was abbot of Lastingham and the brother of Cedd. It will be remembered that King Oswy had chosen Cedd to work among the East Saxon people and it is likely that he still favoured the Celtic Church and took the opportunity, during Wilfrid's absence, to appoint Chad to work in his kingdom. It was Oswy's son Alchfrid, who as sub-king of Deira had, in the first place, with his father's consent, sent his friend Wilfrid to France for episcopal ordination, wishing him to return to England to serve as his bishop for Alchfrid was a staunch supporter of Roman Christianity and had learnt the Faith from Wilfrid. But Oswy had received his religious training from Celtic monks and Celtic Christianity was still strong in the north. Wilfrid had been appointed to York after his success at the Council of Whitby but now that he was in France, King Oswy and the Celtic clergy had time to reconsider the appointment. Chad was known by all to be a most humble and devout man and a teacher of extraordinary power. His appointment and consecration were quite irregular and uncanonical and later, when Theodore was archbishop, Chad humbly submitted to reconsecration; but for three years he faithfully served the Church in Northumbria while the greatly wronged Wilfrid resumed his life as abbot of Ripon, and carried out episcopal duties for King Wulfhere of Mercia and for King Egbert of Kent.

It would be out of place here to recount in detail the vicissitudes of Wilfrid's eventful and stormy life, but a summary of those events leading up to his work in Sussex may not be out of place. The statesmanlike Archbishop Theodore redressed the wrong done to Wilfrid and restored him to York, appointing Chad to Lichfield. For nine years Wilfrid worked with great zeal and energy in the northern church but when hostility broke out between King Egfrid and himself in connection with the king's marriage he was deprived of his bishopric. Theodore took the opportunity of implementing his programme of reform and he split the large Northumbrian see into three parts, each with its own bishop. Wilfrid, for the first time in the history of the English Church, made an appeal to the Apostolic See of Rome and brought back from Pope Agatho papal documents regarding his irregular removal from office, the pope recommending his restoration to York and the division of the diocese on the condition that the division had the full support of Wilfrid himself, who was to choose his own coadjutors. But King Egfrid and his counsellors and certain clergy rejected the pope's document and accused Wilfrid of having obtained it by bribery. King Egfrid confiscated all the land and property which he himself had once given to Wilfrid, cast him into a dismal prison and forbade his friends to visit him. All this, Wilfrid bore with great humility and fortitude. When, after a year, he was released, he fled southwards knowing that the king's antagonism towards him still smouldered. With a few faithful followers he came to Mercia, Wessex and finally to Sussex where the people were still worshipping pagan gods.

Wilfrid had heard that Ethelwalh, the king of the South Saxons, had received Christian baptism due to the influence of King Wulfhere of Mercia who stood as his godfather and as a token of their friendship Wulfhere had given him the Isle of Wight and land in eastern Hampshire. Ethelwalh's wife was also a Christian and there may have been other Christians among the King's courtiers and noblemen. But after the failure of Dicul and his Celtic monks to convert the South Saxon people no other missionary had entered this isolated kingdom. The door now was open to Wilfrid. He would present himself at the royal court and hope to win the favour and support of King Ethelwalh.

The year was 681 and Wilfrid was forty-seven years old. His reception at the court was cordial. Ethelwalh was charmed by his sincerity, his keen mind and his handsome looks. When he had listened to his story and heard about his exile and sufferings he made a pact of friendship with Wilfrid which, he declared, nothing should have power to break. He also gave him permission to preach the Faith to his people. So Wilfrid's task of evangelizing Sussex began; to help him he had four priests, Eappa, Padda, Burghelm and Oiddi who had accompanied him on his journey from the north.

The success of his mission was due not only to his personal qualities of character, his organizing ability and the eloquence of his preaching but also to his practical wisdom, for he cared not only for the souls of his flock but for their bodies also. He had arrived in Sussex at a time when many of the population were dying of starvation for little rain had fallen during the past few seasons and the crops were failing miserably. The people supplemented their meagre diet by catching eels from the pools and rivers but they knew nothing of sea fishing. It was Bishop Wilfrid who taught them this skill. His band of helpers collected a number of eel nets from the people and Wilfrid and his companions showed them how to cast them into the sea. When later the nets were drawn in they were found to be full of fishes of all kinds. These were divided between the families who had lent the nets, the poor peasant folk and Wilfrid's own company. Bede tells us that by this good deed Wilfrid won the hearts of these ignorant people who now listened with more eagerness to his teaching about the Christian God. Eventually a day was appointed for the baptism of those who believed and on that day, most wonderful to relate, a sweet and gentle rain fell and refreshed the parched earth giving a rich and fruitful season. So the men of Sussex came to understand that God had bestowed upon them spiritual and material blessings and the work of the Church prospered in the kingdom.

In all his efforts to evangelize the South Saxons Wilfrid received the patronage of King Ethelwalh who gave him a large estate on the Selsey peninsular. Here the bishop founded a monastery and from this base carried out his pastoral ministry for a period of five years. He appointed Eappa, the priest, to preside over the monastery as abbot. In addition to the land, Wilfrid received from the king all the property and souls that went with it. One of his first acts of Christian charity was to free the large number of slaves who lived and worked on various parts of the Selsey estate.

Nothing now can be seen of Wilfrid's original monastic site and episcopal seat for it is submerged by the sea, though Camden, in

Britannia, relates that at the end of the eighteenth century traces of buildings were visible at low tide; these, though on the same site as Wilfrid's monastery, would have been of a later date than the seventh century. The five years which Wilfrid spent in Sussex must have been a quiet and welcome interlude in his turbulent career for in 686 when he left there to return to his northern diocese of York more troubles awaited him. The Church in Sussex which he had founded was subsequently ruled by Haedi, bishop of Winchester in the kingdom of Wessex. After Haedi's death in 705 the Wessex see was divided and later it was agreed that the Church in Sussex should no longer be subject to Wessex but should have a bishop of its own as it had done when Bishop Wilfrid first came to convert the kingdom. In 709 Eadbert, abbot of Selsey, was consecrated bishop of the South Saxon people. It was not until 1075 that the cathedral church of Sussex was moved from the small village of Selsey to the more important town of Chichester and here it stands today.

The last we hear of Wilfrid's patron and benefactor, King Ethelwalh, is of his death in 686 at the hands of a young prince of Wessex, Cadwalla who was contending for political supremacy. In 685 he gained this supremacy and Sussex and the Isle of Wight came under his suzerainty. He gave a quarter of the Isle of Wight which was still heathen, to Wilfrid who subsequently transferred the grant to his nephew, a cleric named Bernwini. Wilfrid sent a priest, Hiddila to assist Bernwini in preaching the Faith to the heathen inhabitants of the island. Thus, through the missionary zeal and foresight of Bishop Wilfrid, the Isle of Wight as well as Sussex received the Christian Faith.

A number of early charters relating to the South Saxon kingdom and Selsey minster have survived, which mention names of kings and queens, otherwise unknown, who were apparently ruling simultaneously in Sussex towards the end of the seventh and the beginning of the eighth centuries. A king of the Isle of Wight is mentioned by Bede which suggests that there may have been many other such minor kingdoms in early Anglo-Saxon England each with its own ruler who was subject to an overlord according to which major kingdom was dominant at the time. The Isle of Wight during this period came successively under the control of the kingdoms of Mercia, Sussex and Wessex.

Selsey minster, like many other religious houses of the seventh century, was subjected to a severe outbreak of plague from which a number of the brethren, including some of the new recruits, died. Bede records a story told to him by his friend Acca, bishop of Hexham, in connection with this outbreak. The brethren, he says, were so distressed at the deaths of their companions and so fearful that the sickness might claim more of their numbers that they attempted to avert the plague by observing a three day fast to be accompanied by earnest prayer for their survival. On the second day of the fast a young Saxon boy who had joined the community, and now lay dying from the sickness, was granted a vision of the Apostles. The two chief Apostles, Peter and Paul, bade him put away all fear of death for the joys of heaven, they said, were in store for him. He was charged to send for the priest Eappa and to tell him that the prayers of the brethren had been heard and that no more deaths would occur in the monastery. They were to end their fast and give thanks for this answer to their prayer which had been granted through the intercession of the devout King Oswald, once ruler of Northumbria and overlord of all the southern kingdoms. The child then called for Eappa and related the vision to him, describing the appearance of the Apostles, their clothes and the beauty and kindness of their faces. Eappa ordered the fast to be broken, a meal to be prepared and masses to be said in thanksgiving for the preservation of their lives and in honour of St Oswald whose feast day it was that very day. The child, who was of an innocent and gentle disposition received his last Communion and died peacefully, but all the other sick brethren recovered. This incident, says Bede, induced many to put their trust in prayer and the "wholesome remedy of fasting."

W E HAVE already referred to a branch of monasticism, the Order of Anchorites, which made a strong appeal to certain lofty souls who wished to devote themselves to solitary prayer and ascetic practices. In England such an anchorite within the Celtic Church was Fursey's brother Ultan who left the community at Burgh Castle and in a remote part of East Anglia lived his solitary life of prayer, fasting and manual labour. But anchorites were known also within the Roman Church and St Benedict in his Rule says of them, "having learnt in association with many brethren how to fight against the devil, (they) go out well-armed from the ranks of the community to the solitary combat of the desert. They are able now to live without the help of others, and by their own strength and God's assistance to fight against the temptations of mind and body."*

England's most celebrated anchorite within the Roman Church of the Conversion period was Guthlac of Crowland who, in the dank and dismal marshes of Lincolnshire, rose to such heights of sanctity that he was permitted to hold discourse with angels and was sought out by many mortal men who desired to benefit from his wisdom.

Guthlac rightly belongs to the history of Mercia, a kingdom not covered in any detail in this book, but his connections and those of his biographer with East Anglia are strong enough to justify the inclusion of a chapter on this gentle, charming and eccentric saint. Crowland, the scene of his activities, was in territory which lay between East Anglia and Mercia. It was in a kingdom known as Middle Anglia whose inhabitants lived in the valleys of the Welland, Nene and Ouse and which in Guthlac's time was under the domination of Mercia. East Anglians came to visit the saint at Crowland and it was a king of East Anglia, Aelfwald, ruling from 713 to 749, who commissioned the writing of his *Life*. The writer of the Latin Life was the monk Felix, not to be confused with Bishop Felix, Apostle of East Anglia. Felix the monk was most

*The Rule of St Benedict. Translated J. McCann.

likely a native of East Anglia and attached to a monastery either in that kingdom or in Mercia. In the Prologue to his work he refers to King Aelfwald as "beloved by me beyond any other of royal rank" which suggests some kind of personal connection with Aelfwald's kingdom. He wrote his biography of Guthlac towards the middle of the eighth century, possibly between 730 and 740.*

Readers of Felix's *Life of Guthlac* and Bede's *Life of Cuthbert,* an earlier work, cannot fail to notice the similarity between the two biographies, so close in parts that they are verbally identical. Felix evidently used Bede's work as a pattern for his own, though he lacked the straightforward narrative skill of Bede and wrote his own biography in a complicated and gradiose literary style similar to that of Aldhem, the scholarly abbot of Malmesbury whose writings influenced many scholars of his day. The likeness of Felix's *Life of Guthlac* to Bede's *Life of Cuthbert,* to Athanasius' *Life of Anthony* and to a number of other popular *Saints' Lives* is too close to make the genuine origin of much of Felix's material credible and we may surmise that the work contains elements of pure fabrication, included, no doubt, to interest and edify his readers and to enhance the virtues of the saint. But Felix's *Life of Guthlac,* makes entertaining reading and apart from the either borrowed or invented material there is much of value in the work, particularly in its historical details and there are passages in it of singular charm.

Guthlac was born in 674. Three kings ruled Mercia during his lifetime: Ethelred, brother of Wulfhere came to the throne in 674 and ruled for thirty years. In 704 he resigned the kingdom and received the tonsure at Bardney monastery in Lincolnshire. He was succeeded by his nephew, Coenred, who after a short reign of five years made a pilgrimage to Rome, received the tonsure and remained there until the end of his life. The Mercian throne in 709 now devolved upon Ceolred, Ethelred's son, who had previously been passed over in favour of Coenred. Boniface, the English missionary in Germany, described Ceolred as a man of debauched character, disobedient to the laws of God and oppressive towards the Church.†
He was still ruling Mercia in 714 when Guthlac died, but two

---

*Felix's *Life of Guthlac*. Edited and translated by Bertram Colgrave, from which all quotations in this chapter are taken. See also two Anglo-Saxon poems on Guthlac in *Anglo-Saxon Poetry*. Translated R. K. Gordon.

†*English Historical Documents*. Volume I. Number 177.

years later he was succeeded by a young prince whom he had driven into exile, Aethelbald, grandson of Penda's brother and a claimant to the Mercian throne. We shall see later that Aethelbald while in exile was a frequent visitor to Guthlac's hermitage at Crowland.

Guthlac's parents, Tette his mother and Penwalh his father, who was descended from the royal house of Mercia, were devout Christians. The birth of their son, like that of other saints, was heralded by strange and wonderful portents. Before the event, a hand of dazzling brightness, which in early Christian imagery represented God, was seen to issue from the clouds, marking the door of the house where the child was to be born. All men wondered at this sign and at the hour of his birth a woman in attendance came from the house with words of prophecy on her lips. "Stand still, for a man child who is destined to future glory has been born into this world," she said.

The infant was baptized and named Guthlac. He grew up to be a paragon of childhood virtue, gentle, obedient and dutiful, displaying none of the coarse manners and petulent ways of other children. At an early age he was captivated by the music of the minstrels and the songs of his nation's heroes and their bravery in battle and as he grew up into early manhood he aspired to imitate those deeds of valour. At fifteen or so he embarked upon a military career, and joined bands of raiders who attacked cities and villages. Soon he rose to positions of leadership and acquired great skill in battle gathering vast quantities of spoil from the defeated enemy; but always he restored a third of the spoil to the owners. For nine years Guthlac pursued this course of action inflicting heavy losses upon the enemy and gaining for himself immense treasure.

At the age of twenty-four, when his enemies were recovering from recent onslaughts, Guthlac had time to reflect on his victories and the bloody battles and slaughter in which he had shared. He reflected too upon the past history of Mercia, upon its leaders and heroes and its kings who had perished so wretchedly in battle. His own experience on the battlefield had been a constant reminder to him of the transience of human life; death awaited him as it awaited every man. He began to recall the truths of the Faith in which he had been nurtured and to consider to what purpose he was wasting his years acquiring riches and earthly glory which must all pass away in death. He thought perhaps of those other heroes of Mercia and of the neighbouring kingdoms of the English, spiritual heroes like the saintly Bishop Chad who had preached the Faith in Mercia, of Fursey the Irish monk of Cnobheresburg in East Anglia and his brother Ultan the anchorite, of Botolph at Icanhoh and Bishop Wilfrid, his contemporary and friend of Mercia's King Ethelred. How much better, thought Guthlac, to imitate such men as these, than violent and rapacious warriors like Penda. A spiritual flame kindled within Guthlac's heart and his way became clear; the days of his military warfare were over. He would renounce for ever the pomp and riches of this world and spend his remaining years in spiritual warfare and service of his heavenly Lord. So Guthlac abandoned his military career, resolutely brushed aside every objection and impediment to his plan, forsook all his possessions and made his way to Mercia's great minster at Repton where many monks and nuns were ruled by the Abbess Aelfthryth.

At Repton he received the Roman form of tonsure. He studied the monastic Rule, the chanting of psalms and prayers, he read the Scriptures and the *Lives of the Saints* and he strove daily to atone for his past sins. He refused to take any intoxicating drink which at first antagonised his fellow monks but soon he won the affection of all by his sincerity, modesty and gentle ways. Felix describes him at this time as "distinguished in appearance, chaste of body, handsome of face, devout in mind." He stayed at Repton for two years, endeavouring always to cultivate in himself the good qualities of character which he saw in his companions. He was greatly influenced by his reading of the *Lives of the Saints* and in particular the *Lives of the Desert Fathers* who, like Antony of Egypt and countless others had sought to escape from the distractions of the world and to live in solitude, devoting themselves to study, prayer and mortification. Guthlac, too, possessed the inward tranquility, the unshakeable faith and the strength of character to qualify him for such a mode of life. He resolved to become an anchorite.

In 699 he gained the consent of the abbess and his other superiors at Repton to leave the monastery in order to live in some secluded place. He travelled eastwards until he struck the fenland swamps that lay between Mercia and East Anglia in the kingdom of Middle Anglia. The region is, today, one of rich farmland but in Guthlac's time it was a wild, undrained quagmire which Felix describes as "a very long tract, now consisting of marshes, now of bogs, sometimes of black waters overhung by fog, sometimes studded with wooded islands and traversed by the windings of tortuous streams." A more desolate spot he could not have found nor one more suitable for the exercise of spiritual warfare for it was reported that the fens were haunted by demons and that no one before Guthlac had dared to live on the remote island of Crowland in the heart of this marshy swamp. Guthlac heard of the island from a local inhabitant, Tatwine, who escorted him there in a fisherman's skiff. The saint was immediately drawn to the place and believing that God had brought him there he decided to build his hermitage on the island. His preliminary visit to Crowland was a short one for he wished first to return to Repton to take his final leave of the brethren, to encourage them in their communal life in the monastery and to tell them of the place he had chosen for a hermitage. He was back again at Crowland on 24th August 699, never more to leave it. The day was the Feast of St Bartholomew the Apostle who in future was to be his heavenly guardian and helper. For a dwelling Guthlac converted what appeared to be a pre-historic or Roman grave mound which was partly open to the sky for at one time thieves had broken into it hoping to find treasure. Over the hole he built a simple hut, part of it serving as an oratory.

Here at Crowland Guthlac lived out his days in prayer and ascetic discipline, clothing himself only in animal skins and feeding on a meagre diet of barley bread and muddy water from the sluggish fenland streams. Little wonder that in this starved condition he should have been assailed by temptations to despair and a prey to wild fancies and hallucinations. Had he undertaken a task too great for his strength he wondered? But Bartholomew, his heavenly companion, appeared, to console and reassure him and never again after this was he tempted to despair. But other temptations assailed him and it seemed one night as if the forces of evil took bodily shape and invaded his cell in the form of hosts of hideous demons. Felix describes these diabolical creatures in picturesque language; "they were ferocious in appearance, terrible in shape, with great heads, long necks, thin faces, yellow complexions, filthy beards. . . twisted jaws, thick lips, strident voices, singed hair. . ." Shrieking and bellowing, they bound Guthlac's limbs and carried him out of his cell, hurling him into the black waters of the marsh and dragging him through briers and thickets, beating and tormenting him. Then in a final effort to break his spirit they carried him to the sulphurous jaws of hell, threatening to hurl him inside; but even this ordeal failed to shake his confidence in God, "Woe unto you, you sons of darkness, seed of Cain, you are but dust and ashes," he said and at that moment Bartholomew appeared in radiant splendour and at his presence the evil spirits began to howl and tremble. He commanded them to cease tormenting Guthlac and to return him to his cell. Meekly they obeyed the Apostle's command and with the utmost gentleness carried the saint back to his hermitage, bewailing their failure to overmaster him. Then they "vanished like smoke from his presence" and as dawn broke Guthlac gave thanks to Christ for his victory.

Many tales survive of the saints' tender concern for birds and animals, classic among them Jerome's concern for the injured lion out of whose paw he extracted a thorn. Cuthbert of Lindisfarne, during a journey, was more anxious about his horse's hunger than his own and when a loaf was found he shared it with the beast. "O God," he said, "I was fasting for love of Thee and in return Thou hast fed both me and my animal, blessed be Thy Name."* So gentle and benign was the influence of the saints that the most savage creatures were subdued by their presence. Columbanus walked fearlessly among them in the wild regions of the Vosges mountains, a ferocious bear quietly obeying him when he ordered it to leave the cave where he wished to pray. Swallows circled fearlessly around Guthlac in his cell and settled on his shoulders and when Abbot Wilfrid showed surprise at their tameness Guthlac replied, "Have you not read how if a man is joined to God in purity of spirit, all things are united to him in God? and he who refuses to be acknowledged by men seeks the recognition of wild beasts and the visitations of angels."

Men of such sanctity as Guthlac were able to heal the sick, but the wonders they performed, like those of Christ himself, are best seen as examples of the efficacy of prayer rather than as mere displays of magical power. "The prayer offered in faith will save the sick man," said James, the New Testament letter writer. Guthlac when confronted by a case of severe mental disturbance took the young East Anglian nobleman, who had been brought to him, by the hand, led him into his oratory and there prayed and fasted for three days; then he baptized him and in accordance with the ancient custom of the Church "breathed into his face the breath of

---

*Lives of the Saints. Penguin Classics.

healing" after which the youth was never again troubled by fits of madness. But contact with Guthlac's clothing also produced miraculous cures. A companion of Prince Aethelbald was instantly healed of his malady when he wound the saint's girdle around himself and Ofa, one of Aethelbald's retainers, recovered from a septic foot when Guthlac laid his sheepskin prayer-rug over him.

Like other solitaries of the desert Guthlac's sanctity soon attracted visitors from the world who came to him for counsel, comfort or healing. From Mercia and beyond came noblemen and peasants, rich and poor, monks and abbots, priests and bishops and none returned without a blessing. Two of his frequent visitors were the priest, Cissa and Wilfrid the abbot. Both men were able, later, to give Felix trustworthy information about Guthlac which provided material for his biography.

Guthlac's most distinguished royal visitor was Prince Aethlebald, a grandson of Penda's brother Eowa, and a claimant to the Mercian throne. He had been driven into exile by the reigning king, Ceolred, an oppressive and dissolute tyrant who feared the claims of this young rival. To Aethelbald, Crowland became a place of peace and refuge where he could confide in Guthlac and benefit from his wise counsel. The saint possessed gifts of prophecy and foretold that the young prince would eventually overcome his political opponents and succeed to the Mercian throne. "Not as booty nor as spoil shall the kingdom be granted you, but you shall obtain it from the hand of God." The words fell like a benediction upon the fugitive prince; he must have remembered them in later years when the prophecy was fulfilled.

At some time during his fifteen years at Crowland, Guthlac received ordination to the priesthood. Headda, bishop of Lichfield in the province of Mercia, came with Wigfrith his secretary and other attendants to visit him. Their discussion on the Scriptures and other religious matters convinced the bishop of Guthlac's genuine sanctity for "there was such a glory of divine grace in Guthlac, the man of God, that whatever he preached seemed as if uttered by the mouth of an angel." The bishop urged Guthlac to receive ordination to the priesthood for, though he had joined a monastic order at Repton, he had never sought priestly ordination; but now he was prepared to comply with the bishop's wishes. Headda consecrated the oratory where Guthlac was accustomed to pray and where in future he would celebrate the Eucharist. Then he ordained Guthlac to the priesthood and dedicated and blessed the island of Crowland. This took place on 21st August and shortly before the Feast of St Bartholomew but the year is not known. Headda had become bishop of Lichfield in 691, about eight years before Guthlac had settled in Crowland, and in 702 he became responsible also for the diocese of Middle Anglia, the region to which Crowland belonged. It is probable then that Headda ordained Guthlac sometime after 702.

In 714 and at the age of forty, Guthlac's wasted body, exhausted by so much fasting and austerity, succumbed to a fatal disease, warning of which came to him as he prayed in his oratory; suddenly he felt overcome by pain and great weakness. His illness lasted for eight days and he died on the Wednesday of Easter week. Felix gives a detailed account of the saint's illness, death, and the translation of his uncorrupt body, an account which strongly resembles Bede's account of the death of Cuthbert, though there are distinctive features in Felix's narrative. During his last days Guthlac was attended by a priest, Beccel, who on Easter Sunday was present in the oratory when Guthlac, despite his weakness, celebrated the Eucharist; after receiving the Sacrament Guthlac, with profound wisdom, preached the Word of God to Beccel. When he knew that the saint's end was near Beccel ventured to enquire of him who it was who had conversed with him every morning and evening for Beccel had often heard Guthlac talking with an unseen guest. Guthlac told him that soon after he had come to live at Crowland, God had sent an angel to converse with him, to console him and "to relieve the hardness of my toil."

Guthlac's body was buried in the oratory close to his hermitage; it was wrapped first in a linen shroud and placed in a leaden coffin, both of which had been given to him during his lifetime by the Abbess Ecgburgh who was the daughter of King Aldwulf of the East Angles. This king was a nephew of the celebrated abbess of Whitby, Hilda, for his mother, Hereswith, was Hilda's sister. It was this king also who remembered seeing King Redwald's pagan temple, in which he erected an altar to Christ alongside one devoted to pagan deities. But of Aldwulf's daughter, Ecgburgh the nun, we have no further information other than that given by Felix in his *Life of Guthlac,* and this refers only to her gift of the coffin and shroud to Guthlac and an enquiry she made of the saint as to who would succeed him at Crowland.

Guthlac's death was a cause of deep distress to Prince Aethelbald; in his grief he visited the saint's grave, prostrating himself before it, praying and weeping, "My father, you know my wretchedness, you have always been my helper. . . now whither shall I turn my face? whence shall come help, and who, most excellent father, will give me counsel?" That night as Aethelbald lay in the hut where he was accustomed to lodge during his visits to Crowland, he was consoled by a vision of the saint standing before him in radiant splendour. Guthlac bade him put away his grief and fears for soon, he said, his sufferings and exile would be ended and he would receive the royal sceptre; as a sign of the truth of this prophecy Guthlac told him that in the morning, unhoped-for food would be brought to the island for the relief of those who dwelt there. All that Aethelbald had been told by Guthlac in the vision came to pass, for next morning there came the sound of the island's signal, a bell or some such device, which Guthlac had erected at the landing-stage to warn him of the approach of visitors. When Aethelbald learned that unexpected strangers had brought food to the island his belief in Guthlac's prophecies was confirmed and he felt greatly encouraged by this sign. A year later, in 716, when King Ceolred died, Aethelbald succeeded to the Mercian throne, his reign covering a period of forty years. Bede speaks of him as a powerful king and overlord of all the southern kingdoms.

In a letter to Aethelbald, Boniface, the English missionary to the Germans, praises him for his social justice, his maintenance of peace and generosity in almsgiving. But the letter reveals a shadier side to the king's character which may have developed later in his life, for the letter was not written until 746. In it he is reproved by Boniface for appropriating to himself certain monastic revenues and for immoral conduct which he says is unseemly in one of his rank and position. He is urged to live in lawful marriage and to avoid the snares of Satan into which his predecessor Ceolred had fallen. "Therefore I beg, most dear son, that instructed by these admonitions, you assent to the wholesome words of the law of God and amend your life. Abandon vices, and be zealous in the practice of holy virtues."* Although it is clear from the letter that Aethelbald had deprived churches and monasteries of their revenues a number of charters indicate that he also granted privileges to the Church and made donations of land for the establishment of monasteries. He was, as Dr

---

*English Historical Documents. Volume I. Number 177.

Wallace-Hadrill says, equivocal, "what he gave with one hand he took back with the other."* Ten years after the letter was written he was treacherously murdered at Seckington near Tamworth by men of his own bodyguard. We may wonder why no hint of Aethelbald's moral laxity is shown in Felix's *Life of Guthlac*. If Felix knew of it, his biography of Guthlac was no place in which to draw attention to it, for the *Lives of the Saints* were written for the edification of their readers, monks and nuns and in this case for Aelfwald, king of East Anglia, a kingdom under the control of Mercia. When Felix wrote his biography Aethelbald was not yet dead. It would hardly have been wise to portray Aethelbald in any other than a favourable light. In the *Life of Guthlac,* Moreover, Aethelbald was a young man, a fugitive and an exile, without political position or power and at the time, no doubt, morally blameless; only later, in the days of his prosperity and after his rise to power did the moral decline most likely set in.

The existence of an abbey at Crowland at the beginning of the eleventh century is historically certain but the precise date of its foundation, which may have been as early as the eighth century, is not known. Felix relates that a year after Guthlac's death his body was exhumed and found to be uncorrupt. It was not reburied in the earth but placed in a monumental shrine which King Aethelbald enriched and ornamented; but there is no reference to his having founded an abbey there. Whatever the date of its foundation it owes its true origin to the saint who first inhabited this deserted and demon-infested swamp and sanctified it by his prayers, fasts and vigils. His name in later years was to form part of the triple dedication of Crowland's medieval abbey; the north aisle of the church still stands today and serves as the parish church of Crowland. A few miles from Crowland is the village of Market Deeping which once belonged to Crowland Abbey. Its church is one of the nine in England, four in Lincolnshire, two in Leicestershire, two in Northamptonshire and one in Bedfordshire dedicated to St Guthlac. In the chancel, scenes from his life are depicted in the nineteenth century stained glass window. These were copied from the Guthlac Roll in the British Museum, a parchment roll of some nine feet long, on which are drawn, with great beauty and delicacy of design, eighteen scenes, though there may originally have been more, from the saint's life: his journey

---

Early Germanic Kingship in England and on the Continent.

by boat to Crowland, his receiving the tonsure, his ordination by Bishop Headda and so on.* The roll dates from the end of the twelfth century and may have been produced at Crowland Abbey, possibly as a basis for some designs for a series of stained glass windows for the Abbey Church, which, if they were ever executed, could have perished in the Cromwellian reform movement of the seventeenth century. It is of interest also to find mentioned in an eleventh century will and in Doomsday Book, a church of secular canons, dedicated to St Guthlac at Hereford, a considerable distance from Crowland.

One may ask, in conclusion, what distinctive contribution the anchorite saints, such as Guthlac, made towards the growth and development of the Church, for unlike Botolph, Fursey or Wilfrid, they trained no community of monks, founded no monasteries, built no churches and conducted no preaching missions. Their contribution must be measured in spiritual rather than in practical terms for they were, above all else, men of prayer and deep spiritual devotion. The undercurrent of spirituality which pervades life and of which most of us are only intermittently aware, was to them the true reality. They lived at a depth undreamed of by the majority of men and followed their Lord with a zeal and passion of soul known to few. By their pursuit of moral goodness, by their poverty, renunciation and humility they demonstrated to the world a standard of values the very antithesis of its own, reminding men that among all the vicissitudes and pressures of human life, their true destiny is a spiritual one.

By their withdrawal from the society of men the anchorite saints emphasised the primary and ultimate importance of man's relationship with God, compared to which, his relationship with his fellow men, though highly significant and meaningful, is secondary and relative. "Except a man shall say in his heart, I alone and God are in the world, he shall find no peace," said the abbot Allois.† The anchorites' purpose in withdrawing from the world was not in order to avoid the tensions which living within it involves, for usually they had learnt first to live peaceably among men, but in order to cultivate that friendship with God which is the chief purpose of man's life on earth. "He who is often

---

*British Museum. Harl. Roll. Y.6.

† Introduction. *The Desert Fathers.* Helen Waddell.

visited by men cannot be often visited by angels," said Guthlac, and here perhaps lies the secret of the anchorites' capacity to endure prolonged periods of solitude.

Bibliography

Roman Britain

Birley, A. *Life in Roman Britain.* 1964.
Collingwood and Myres. *Roman Britain and the English Settlements.* 1937.
Liversidge, J. *Britain in the Roman Empire.* 1968.
Richmond, I. A. *Roman Britain.* 1955.

The Anglo-Saxons

Sources
Anglo-Saxon Chronicle. Translated G. N. Garmonsway 1960.
Bede's *Ecclesiastical History of the English People.*
   i) Edited B. Colgrave and R. A. B. Mynors 1969.
   ii) Translated L. Sherley-Price, Penguin Classics 1955.
   iii) Latin Text and Notes C. Plummer 1896.
English Historical Documents. Vol. 1. Edited D. Whitelock. 1955.
Laws of the Earliest English Kings. F. L. Attenborough. 1922.

General
Hodgkin, R. K. *A History of the Anglo-Saxons.* 1952.
Hunter-Blair, P. *An Introduction to Anglo-Saxon England.* 1956.
Hunter-Blair, P. *Roman Britain and Early England.* 1963.
Loyn, H. R. *Anglo-Saxon England and the Norman Conquest.* 1962.
Page, R. I. *Life in Anglo-Saxon England,* 1970.
Stenton, F. *Anglo-Saxon England.* 1947.
Whitelock, D. *The Beginnings of English Society.* 1952.

The Church — Roman and Celtic

Chadwick, N. *The Age of Saints in the Early Celtic Church.* 1961.
Deanesly, M. *The Pre-Conquest Church in England.* 1963.
Deanesly, M. *Augustine of Canterbury.* 1964.
Duckett, E. S. *Anglo-Saxon Saints and Scholars.* 1947.
Godfrey, C. J. *The Church in Anglo-Saxon England.* 1962.
Hughes, K. *The Church in Early Irish Society.* 1966.
Hunter-Blair, P. *The World of Bede.* 1970.
De Paor, M. and L. *Early Christian Ireland.* 1958.
Williams, H. *Christianity in Early Britain.* 1912.

Saints' Lives
Original Sources
Benedict. *The Dialogues of Gregory.* Edited E. G. Gardner. 1911.
Columbanus. *Sancti Columbani Opera.* G. S. M. Walker. 1957.
Germanus. *The Western Fathers.* F. R. Hoare. 1954.
Guthlac, Felix's Life of. Translated B. Colgrave. 1956.
Wilfrid, Eddius Stephanus Life of. Translated B. Colgrave. 1927.

Saints' Lives

General
Attwater, D. *The Penguin Dictionary of Saints.* 1965.
Butler. *Lives of the Saints.* Revised H. Thurston and D. Attwater. 1956.
Duckett, E. S. *The Wandering Saints.* 1959.
Gould, S. Baring. *The Lives of the Saints.* 1898.
Webb, J. F. *Lives of the Saints.* Penguin Classics. 1965.

Saints in Church Art

Anderson, M. D. *History and Imagery in British Churches.* 1971.
Anderson, M. D. *The Imagery of British Churches.* 1955.
Bell, Mrs Nancy R. *The Saints in Christian Art.* 1901.
Cautley, H. M. *Norfolk Churches.* 1949.
Cautley, H. M. *Suffolk Churches and Their Treasures.* 1937.
Milburn, R. L. P. *Saints and their Emblems in English Churches.* 1957.
Needham, A. *How To Study an Old Church.* 1944.

Church Dedications

Bond, F. *Dedications and Patron Saints of English Churches.* 1914.
Forster, F. Arnold. *Studies in Church Dedications.* 1899.

Anglo-Saxon Art, Architecture and Archaeology

Bruce-Mitford, R. *The Sutton Hoo Ship Burial.* 1947.
Bruce-Mitford, R. *The Sutton Hoo Ship Burial.* British Museum. 1972.
Green, C. *Sutton Hoo.* 1963.
Harden, D. B. *Dark Age Britain.* 1956.
Kendrick, T. D. *Anglo-Saxon Art to AD 900.* 1938.
Taylor, H. M. & J. *Anglo-Saxon Architecture.* 1965.
Wilson, D. *The Anglo-Saxons.* Revised Pelican edition. 1971.

Local History

Bentham, J. *History and Antiquities of Ely.* 1771.
Clarke, R. Rainbird. *East Anglia.* 1960.
Dahl, L. H. *The Roman Camp and the Irish Saint at Burgh Castle.* 1913.
James, M. R. *Norfolk and Suffolk.* 1930.
Routledge, C. F. *St Martin's Church, Canterbury.* 1891.
Stanley, A. P. *Historical Memorials of Canterbury.* 1904.
Victoria County Histories.

Miscellaneous

Decarreaux, J. *Monks and Civilization.* 1964.
Duckett, E. S. *Gateway to the Middle Ages.* 1938.
Gordon, R. K. *Anglo-Saxon Poetry.* 1954.
Hadden and Stubbs. *Councils and Ecclesiastical Documents.* Revised 1964.
Hall, D. J. *English Medieval Pilgrimage.* 1965.
Hole, C. *English Shrines and Sanctuaries.* 1954.
McCann, J. *The Rule of St Benedict.* 1952.
Vermaseren, M. J. *Mithras the Secret God.* 1963.
Wormald, F. *The Miniatures in the Gospels of St Augustine.* 1954.

Index

A

Acca, bishop of Hexham, 119, 125.
Adamnan, abbot of Iona, 75.
Aecci, bishop of Dommoc, 65.
Aelfwald, king of East Anglia, 126, 135.
Aethelbald, king of Mercia, 127, 131, 132–135.
Agatho, Pope, 121.
Aidan, St, 56, 68, 109, 119.
Alban, martyr, 15–17, 24, 89.
Albinus, abbot of Canterbury, 32, 55.
Alchfrid, king of Deira, 121.
Aldhelm, abbot of Malmesbury, 53, 74, 116, 127.
Aldwulf, king of East Anglia, 82, 133.
Ambrosius Aurelianus, 25.
Anchorites, 72, 126, 129, 136, 137.
Anglo-Saxon Chronicle, 25, 32, 64, 66, 67, 88, 90, 92, 93.
Anglo-Saxons, 22–33.
Anna, king of East Anglia, 63–65, 72, 78, 79, 88, 93, 97.
Archaeology, 14, 16, 17–20, 25, 26, 28, 50, 51, 55, 56, 69, 70.
Arles, council of, 15.
Arthur, 25.
Augustine, archbishop of Canterbury, 35–49, 55.
Augustine's Abbey, 44.
Augustine's Gospels, 43.

B

Babingly church, 61.
Badon Hill, 25.
Badwin, bishop of Elmham, 65.
Barking monastery, 113, 115, 116.
Bartholomew, St, 130, 131.
Beccel, 133.

Bede, 15–18, 24, 30–32, 77, 78, 80, 127.
Benedict, St, 97–99.
Benedictine Rule, 34, 84, 90, 92, 95–97, 99–104, 120, 126.
Bertgils, bishop of East Anglia, 65.
Bertha, queen of Kent, 17, 35, 38, 49.
Bertwald, archbishop of Canterbury, 52, 116.
Bishops, Celtic & Roman, 71, 72.
Bisi, bishop of East Anglia, 65.
Blythborough, Suffolk, 64, 70, 71.
Bobbio, monastery, 59.
Boniface, missionary to the Germans, 51, 52, 127, 134.
Bosham, Sussex, 118.
Boston, Lincs, 93, 95.
Botolph, St, 92–97.
Bradwell-on-Sea, Essex, 109, 110.
Bretwalda, 27, 37, 59, 80.
Bridget, St, 83.
Brythnoth, abbot of Ely, 87, 91.
Burgh Castle, 63, 69.
Bury St Edmunds, 63, 95.

C

Cadwalla, king of Wessex, 124.
Cambridge, 85, 86.
Canterbury, 17, 18, 30, 31, 38, 39, 44, 45, 48, 49, 53, 92, 106.
Canute, king, 87.
Cedd, St, 109–113.
Cellanus, abbot of Peronne, 74.
Celtic Church, 47, 48, 70–72.
Ceolfrith, abbot of Jarrow, 92, 93, 97.
Ceolred, king of Mercia, 127, 128, 132.
Chad, St, 121, 122.
Chelles monastery, 83, 97.

Chertsey monastery, 113, 114.
Chichester, Sussex, 124.
Christchurch, Canterbury, 17, 44.
Christianity, 12, 13.
Christian Symbols, 18—20.
Cissa, 132.
Claudius, emperor, 10.
Clovis II, king of Franks, 73.
Coenred, king of Mercia, 127.
Colchester, Essex, 10, 95.
Coldingham monastery, 81.
Columbanus, St, 58, 59, 66, 70, 73,
  101, 131.
Constantine, emperor, 15, 17, 19.
Constantius, Priest of Lyons, 23.
Crowland, 129, 130, 132, 133, 135,
  136.
Cuthbert, St, 83, 84, 89, 131.
Cynifrid, physician, 85, 86.

D
Daniel, bishop of Winchester, 118.
Danish invasions, 51, 87, 90, 91.
Dante, poet, 75, 76.
Deben, river, 56.
Dereham, Norfolk, 88—91
Demons, 28, 94, 130, 131.
Dicul, priest, 68, 73, 118.
Dommoc (Dunwich ?), 59—61, 65.
Domneva, abbess of Thanet, 51,
  96, 97.
Drycthelm, monk of Melrose, 75.
Dunstan, archbishop of Canterbury,
  90.

E
Eadbald, king of Kent, 49, 50, 108.
Eadbert, bishop of Selsey, 124.
Eadburg, abbess of Thanet, 51, 52.
Eanswyth, abbess of Folkestone,
  50, 51.
Eappa, abbot of Selsey, 123.
Earconbert, king of Kent, 51, 79.
Earconwald, bishop of London,
  113—116.
Earconwald, minister of Clovis II,
  73, 74.
East Anglia, 55, 56.
Ebba, abbess of Coldingham, 81.
Ecgburg, abbess, 133.

Eddius, biographer of Wilfrid, 82,
  83, 119 ff.
Edgar, King, 90, 95.
Education, 30, 43, 45, 46, 58, 63.
Edwin, king of Northumbria, 49,
  50, 57.
Egbert, king of Kent, 51, 52, 121.
Egfrid, king of Northumbria, 77,
  80—82, 122.
Egric, king of East Anglia, 63.
Elmham, Norfolk, 65.
Ely Cathedral, 77, 82, 83, 88.
Ely Chronicle, 61, 63, 64, 78, 80,
  87.
Ely, Isle of, 79.
Emma, queen, 87.
Emperor worship, 11.
Eormenberg, queen of Northumbria,
  81, 82.
Eorpwald, king of East Anglia, 57,
  58.
Epping forest, 106.
Essex, 106 ff.
Ethelberga, abbess of Lyminge, 49,
  50.
Ethelbert, king of Kent, 37—41, 44,
  46, 47, 49.
Ethelburga, abbess of Barking, 115,
  116.
Etheldreda, abbess of Ely, 32,
  77—88.
Ethelhere, king of East Anglia, 79,
  93, 94.
Ethelred, king of Mercia, 127.
Ethelric, king of East Anglia, 82,
  83.
Ethelwald, king of East Anglia, 80.
Ethelwalh, king of South Saxons,
  122—124.
Eusebius, historian, 13, 15.
Exning, Suffolk, 64, 78.

F
Faremoutier, monastery, 93, 97.
Farne Island, 84.
Felix, biographer of Guthlac, 126 ff.
Felix, bishop of East Anglia, 45, 55,
  58—64, 78.
Felixkirk, Yorks, 62.
Felixstowe, Suffolk, 60, 62.

O

Oswald, king of Northumbria, 125.
Oswy, King of Northumbria, 30, 79, 109, 121.
Owini, steward of Etheldreda, 80, 112.

P

Paganism, Anglo-Saxon, 26–29, 40, 43, 106, 108, 113.
Paul, St, 12.
Paulinus, St, 39, 42, 50.
Pelagian heresy, 20, 21, 23, 24.
Penda, king of Mercia, 73.
Penitential, of Theodore, 28.
Péronne, France, 74, 75.
Peterborough, 90.
Picts, 23, 24.
Pilgrimage, 66, 68.
Pilgrim badges, 87.
Plague, 85, 112, 113, 115, 124, 125.

R

Ramsey abbey, 62, 90.
Reculver, Kent, 52.
Redwald, king of East Anglia, 57.
Relics of Saints, 90, 91, 95.
Rendlesham, Suffolk, 56, 60, 64, 94, 111.
Repton monastery, 129.
Richborough, Kent, 22.
Rochester, Kent, 42, 48.
Roman Britain, 10–21.

S

Sabert, king of East Saxons, 107, 108.
Saethryd, abbess of Faremoutier, 64.
Scots, 23.
Sebbi, king of Essex, 111, 115, 116.
Selby abbey, Yorks, 24.
Selsey, Sussex, 27, 123–125.
Sexburg, abbess of Sheppey and Ely, 51, 85, 86.

Sheppey minster, 51.
Sigbert, king of East Anglia, 58, 59, 63, 64.
Sigbert, king of Essex, 109–111.
Sighere, king of Essex, 111.
Soham, Cambs, 61, 62.
Sussex, 118 ff.
Sutton Hoo, 26, 55, 56, 71.
Swidhelm, king of Essex, 111.

T

Tatwini, 130.
Tertullian, 11, 14, 15, 17.
Thanet, Kent, 38, 39.
Theodore, archbishop of Canterbury, 53, 54, 114, 122.
Thomas, bishop of East Anglia, 65.
Thorney abbey, 92, 93.
Tonbert, prince of Gyrwas, 79.

U

Ultan, brother of Fursey, 68, 72, 73, 76.

V

Vergilius, archbishop of Arles, 42.
Verulamium (St Albans), 16, 17.
Vision literature, 75, 76.
Vortigern, British chieftain, 24.

W

Waldhere, bishop of London, 116.
Wergild, 27.
Whitby synod, 48, 112, 119.
Wiggenhall, Norfolk, 96.
Wight Isle of, 124.
Wilfrid, abbot, 132.
Wilfrid, bishop of York, 78, 80–83, 86, 119–124.
William of Malmesbury, 14.
Wini, bishop of London, 113.
Withburga, abbess of Dereham, 88–91.
Wulfhere, king of Mercia, 113.

Y

Ythancaestir, see Bradwell-on-Sea.

Lup̄ epiſc̄op̄

Bishops Germanus and Lupus in Britain. Germanus carries a casket containing soil stained with th